Bernd Rolff

Shopping For You

Englisch für Auszubildende im Einzelhandel

1. Auflage

Bestellnummer 11315

Haben Sie Anregungen oder Kritikpunkte zu diesem Produkt?
Dann senden Sie eine E-Mail an 11315_001@bv-1.de
Autoren und Verlag freuen sich auf Ihre Rückmeldung.

Bildquellenverzeichnis:
© Fotolia.com: Umschlagfoto (Yuri Arcurs), 17 (moonrun), 68 (Monkey Business), 90 (erdquadrat), 113 (sheldon gardner), 115 (endostock), 134 (Bernhard Richter), 135 (Vitaly Maksimchuk); MEV Verlags GmbH: 55/außer 2. v. u., 74/u., 111; Rolff, Bernd: 35, 53, 54, 55/2. v. u., 72, 73, 74/o., 99; Tesco PLC, Cheshunt, Großbritannien: 28, 31; Bergt, Raimo: Illustrationen (außer S. 117); Wetterauer, Oliver: Illustration 117

www.bildungsverlag1.de

Bildungsverlag EINS GmbH
Sieglarer Straße 2, 53842 Troisdorf

ISBN 978-3-427-**11315**-7

Introduction

Über dieses Buch

„Shopping for you“ wurde speziell für Auszubildende im Einzelhandel entwickelt. Somit liegt der Schwerpunkt auf Tätigkeiten im Lebensmittelbereich/Supermarkt.

Aufbau der Units

Alle Kapitel im Buch sind gleich strukturiert. Die Abschnitte 1 (Section 1) enthalten pro Kapitel (Unit) zwei Texte mit den dazugehörigen Vokabeln. Das Kapitel schließt mit einer Verständnisübung ab. Im ersten Abschnitt der Kapitel liegt der Fokus auf umfangreichen und zusammenhängenden Texten. Die Handlungen basieren auf der beruflichen Realität, sie sind logisch und verständlich strukturiert, sie bauen aufeinander auf, und die Texte bieten aufgrund ihres Umfangs genügend Übungsstoff, unter anderem auch für die heutzutage häufig vernachlässigten Diktate. Die wichtigsten Vokabeln befinden sich jeweils in der Reihenfolge ihres Vorkommens direkt unter den Texten. Damit wird das Nachschlagen im Vokabelteil des Buches während der Bearbeitung der Texte weitgehend vermieden. Trotzdem gibt es im Anhang des Buches auch einen alphabetisch geordneten Vokabelteil Deutsch-Englisch/Englisch-Deutsch. Im ersten Abschnitt des Buches werden die erforderlichen Erklärungen durchweg in englischer Sprache gegeben. Die Lernenden werden damit regelmäßig aufgefordert, die im Anhang des Buches aufgeführten sehr umfangreichen Vokabellisten zu verwenden.

Im zweiten Kapitel wird die Fachkunde thematisiert. Auch dieses Kapitel ist fast durchgehend in englischer Sprache abgefasst, damit die Lernenden sich auch hier mit dem Vokabelteil des Buches befassen. Dieser Abschnitt vermittelt alle für die Tätigkeit erforderlichen Begriffe der Fachkunde.

Im jeweils dritten Abschnitt der Kapitel wird eine kurze Grammatikwiederholung angeboten, die aber ohne Weiteres ausgelassen werden kann, wenn es der Wissensstand der Schüler erlaubt. In diesem Teil sind die Erklärungen hauptsächlich deutsch, da die Schüler hier selbstständig arbeiten sollen.

Der vierte und letzte Teil des Buches bietet im Kapitel "Practise your word power" jeweils eine Reihe von Vokabelübungen an, die gleich strukturiert sind, und in denen hauptsächlich die im jeweiligen Kapitel vorkommenden Fachvokabeln wiederholt bzw. vertieft werden.

Zusätzlich zur eigentlichen Bestimmung als Lehrbuch für die Berufsschule eignet sich "Shopping for you" aber auch für den Einzelhandelskaufmann nach Abschluss der Ausbildung aufgrund des sehr umfangreichen Fachvokabelteils als Nachschlagewerk bei der täglichen Arbeit. Es ist natürlich auch für das Selbststudium einsetzbar.

Hameln, im Frühjahr 2009

Bernd ROLFF
staatlich geprüfter u. beeidigter Übersetzer BDÜ

Table of Contents

Erklärung der Zeichen und Abkürzungen

i.S.v.	=	*im Sinne von*	
i.d.B.v.	=	*in der Bedeutung von*	*(wird bei englischen Wötern verwendet, die mehrere Bedeutungen haben)*
(U)	=	*Umgangssprache*	
m.S.m.	=	*mehrere Schreibweisen möglich*	
(to, r)	=	*regelmäßiges Verb*	
(to, ir)	=	*unregelmäßiges Verb*	

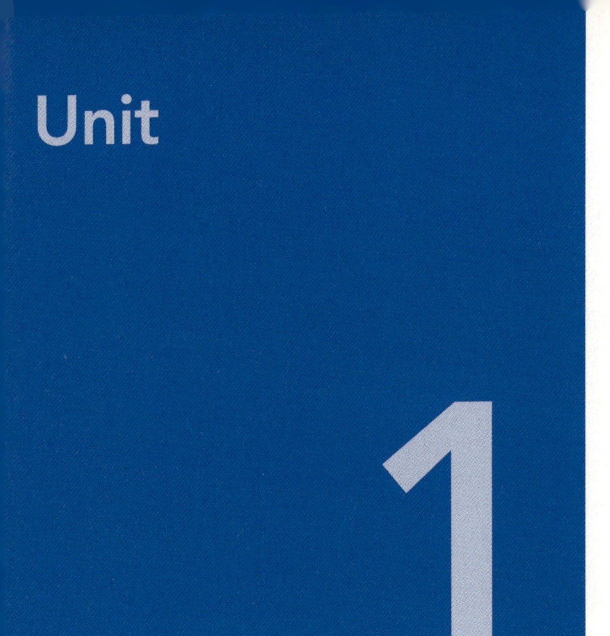

Section 1 Texts

Text 1 A very difficult decision

This afternoon (it's Monday.), Michael is allowed to finish work early because he is on the morning shift this week. He started work at half past six in the morning. The supermarket he works in usually opens at seven o'clock.
Oh sorry, we forgot to introduce Michael. His full name is Michael Crocker, he is 19 years old and he lives in a small town in Lower Saxony in the north of Germany. Michael lives with his parents, they have a house near the army barracks. Michael's father Gordon is an officer in the British army. His mother Renate is German, so Michael grew up bilingual. That means that he can speak English and German fluently. Michael also has two younger sisters named Sharon and Jennifer, but they are not at home with the family: They are in a boarding school in England. Michael, however, went to school in Germany, finished school last year at the age of 18 and then found a job as an assistant in the local SUPRA supermarket, a chain of supermarkets for the British Forces in Germany. He loves to work there because he likes to work with people, and he finds working with customers very interesting. The supermarket he works for is for the British Forces, but Michael absolves a proper apprenticeship under German regulations, and once a week he has to go to the local "Berufsschule" – the vocational training college.

When Michael comes home this afternoon shortly after three o'clock, he sees his father's car parked in front of the house, so his dad is already home. This is unusual because his
25 father often has to work late, and sometimes he is away for a long time because he is on exercise. Michael immediately sees that something unusual must have happened because his father has a letter in his hand which looks very official. What could it be? Now his father tells him that he will have to go back to England: The army has posted him with effect from (wef) 1st of June to a garrison in the south of England, not too far away from
30 London. This is a shock for Michael. He has just begun his training, what would happen to him? Would he have to go to England together with his parents? Would it be better for him to stay in Germany and finish his apprenticeship first? Of course, he could stay with his grandparents (his mother's parents) who live in the same town. But what about all his friends in town and at work? But on the other hand, London is luring! So many questions!
35 All evening, the family sits together and discusses the future.

Vocabulary List

difficult	schwierig
decision	Entscheidung
to be allowed to	dürfen
shift	Schicht
introduce (to, r)	vorstellen, einführen
Lower Saxony	Niedersachsen
barracks	Kaserne
bilingual	zweisprachig
fluently	fließend
boarding school	Internat
apprentice	Auszubildende/r
apprenticeship	das Ausbildungsverhältnis
vocational training college	Berufsschule
immediately	unmittelbar, sofort
official	amtlich, offiziell
post (to, r)	versetzen
wef (abbr.; with effect from)	mit Wirkung vom
garrison	Garnison, mil. Standort
stay (to; r)	bleiben
lure (to; r)	locken

For the irregular verbs in this story which – some of them are in the past tense – please refer to the "ABC of irregular verbs" in the annex of this book.

Text 2 A talk to the boss

It was Tuesday morning at quarter to seven. Michael took his mountain bike and rode to work. The supermarket he works in is only a few minutes away from his home, so he arrived well in time. After he had arrived, he put on his white coat with the company logo which all members of staff in this SUPRA supermarket have to wear. His boss, whose name is Mr John Franklin, was already there, so Michael knocked on the door of his office. The manager asked him to come in which Michael did. His boss then told him to sit down on the chair in front of his desk. Now Michael explained the situation to him. At first, Mr Franklin seemed to be a little disappointed because he would lose a valuable member of his staff. But then he began to smile because obviously he had a very good idea.
"Maybe I can help you, Michael. One of my friends back in the U.K. is the manager of a big supermarket. You are lucky, it is a supermarket not far away from the place where your parents are going to live. If you want I can give him – his name is Willy Wellwood – a ring later this morning and ask him if he has a vacancy (i.e. a position) for a clever young man!" Michael was surprised. He did not expect things to go that well, he expected difficulties. So obviously he was very lucky, and he quickly agreed to Mr Franklin's plan. Mr Franklin also explained to Michael that some things will be different from what he is used to in Germany. There is no apprenticeship, young people simply start a job with a company and learn their skills while they are working. This system is called "training on the job", and there are also no vocational training colleges in Britain. Many companies, of course, run their own training programmes for their staff in order to make them fit for their jobs.
Mr Franklin now told Michael that he would call his friend Mr Wellwood later on that morning. It simply was too early to do it now because in summer the time in the U.K. is an hour behind the German time, and in winter it is even two hours. So Mr Franklin said: "All right Michael, please go back to work. I will let you know as soon as I have a reply from Mr Wellwood." Michael went back to work. This morning he had to help at the cheese counter. He did not like it too much because it was a little bit chilly there because cheese always has to be kept cool. Some hours later, the mobile phone in the pocket of his coat began to ring. He looked at the number on the display, it was his boss. He now pressed the button with the green receiver on it, and then he had his boss on the phone. The message he got now was very good, Mr Franklin told him that Mr Wellwood would give him a chance to work in the supermarket in the U.K.! He was told to see his boss in the afternoon, then he would be given more details on the new job. Michael was over the moon!

Vocabulary List

in time	pünktlich
explain (to; r)	erklären
staff	Belegschaft, Personal
disappointed	enttäuscht
to lose (to, ir)	verlieren
obviously	offensichtlich
vacancy	hier: freie Stelle
surprised (to be)	überrascht sein
U.K. = United Kingdom	Vereinigtes Königreich
reply	Antwort
chilly	kühl
receiver	Telefonhörer
message	Nachricht
detail	Einzelheit
to be over the moon	überglücklich sein

For the irregular verbs in this story which are all in the past tense please refer to the "ABC of irregular verbs" in the annex of this book.

Comprehension exercise

Please answer the following questions in full sentences.

1 Where in Germany does Michael Crocker live at the moment?
2 Michael can speak two languages. How is such an ability called and why is that so?
3 Why was it unusual for Michael's dad to be home early?
4 Think of some reasons why London is a lure for Michael.
5 What do the staff in the SUPRA supermarket wear at work?
6 What are the main differences between the German and the British vocational training methods?
7 Why doesn't Michael like to work at the cheese counter?
8 How do you accept a phone call on a mobile phone?
9 The word "wef" which appears in the first text is an abbreviation, The verb "to abbreviate" means to make a long word short, so the noun "abbreviation" means "Abkürzung" in German. Can you think of any other abbreviations in the English language and their meanings?
10 How would you define the word "vacancy"?

Section 2 Basics of special terminology in retail

Englische Fachbegriffe

2.1 Working with numbers and figures

There are two different kinds of numbers in the English language. These are called "cardinal numbers" and "ordinal numbers".
Cardinal numbers are used for counting things, e. g.: "1 (one), 2 (two), 3 (three), 4 (four) etc. They can also be used for saying the time.
Ordinal numbers are the ones with a full stop behind them, e. g.: 1. (first), 2. (second), 3. (third), 4. (fourth) etc.
Ordinal numbers can also be written like this: 1st, 2nd, 3rd, 4th, 5th etc.
The first three are irregular ones, but then we simply add the ending "th" to the appropriate cardinal number. We need ordinal numbers for saying the date, for example like this:
Today is Wednesday, the 1st of June 2009

Note

21. = the twenty-first = 21st

22. = the twenty-second = 22nd

23. = the twenty-third = 23rd

31. = the thirty-first = 31st

Vocabulary List

cardinal number	Grundzahl
ordinal number	Ordnungszahl
irregular	unregelmäßig
appropriate	entsprechend

2.2 Telling the time

A clock has two hands (an hour hand and a minute hand or a small hand and a large hand) which show us the time on the dial (the dial is a disc which is numbered from one to twelve).
It is important to know that in Great Britain the clock only goes from 1 to 12. The British do not understand times such as 23.20h. In Britain, they would say that it is "twenty minutes past eleven (p.m.)."

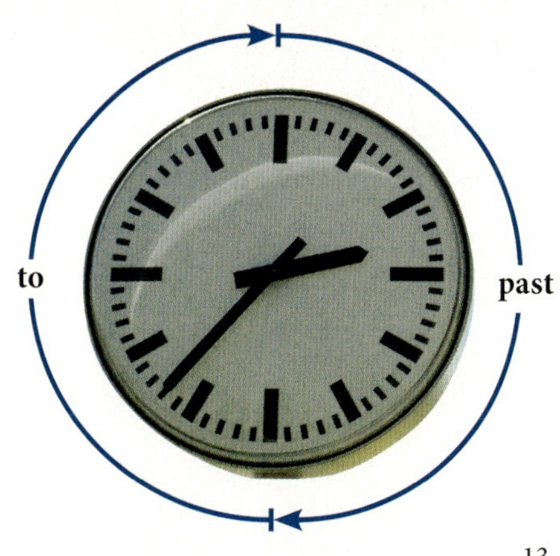

For the first 29 minutes on the dial, we use the word "past", e.g. 11.10h = "ten minutes past eleven". For 30 minutes on the dial, we use the term (word) "half". For the last 29 minutes on the dial, we use the word "to", e.g. 11.50h = "ten minutes to twelve". But in these cases, a little mental arithmetic is sometimes required. If it is, for example, 10.35h, then the British will say: it is 25 minutes to eleven (60 [for the next full hour] – 35 = 25). It is a little bit difficult, but you will soon get used to it.

The only real difference between the German and the British method of saying the time is the half hour. Here is an example for it:

German way of saying:	British way of saying:
11.30h = *Es ist halb zwölf.*	11.30 = It is half past eleven.

(In Deutschland bezieht sich die Angabe der halben Stunde auf die kommende volle Stunde. In Großbritannien dagegen bezieht sich die Angabe der halben Stunde auf die vergangene volle Stunde. Dort sagt man daher wörtlich übersetzt: Es ist „halb nach elf".)

For full hours, we add the word "o'clock", but it is reserved for full hours only.

10.00h = It is ten o'clock.

Fifteen minutes are called "a quarter". So 11.15h is "a quarter past eleven", and 11.45h is "a quarter to twelve".

In order to distinguish between times in the morning and in the afternoon/evening, the British use the abbreviations a.m. and p.m.

These abbreviations, however, are seldom spoken, they are written. Here are two examples:

11.00 a.m. = 11.00 Uhr (morgens)

11.00 p.m. = 23.00 Uhr (abends)

Vocabulary List

clock	die Uhr, die große Uhr
watch	Armbanduhr
dial	Ziffernblatt
hour hand	Stundenzeiger, kleiner Uhrzeiger
minute hand	Minutenzeiger, großer Uhrzeiger
e.g. – for example	zum Beispiel
mental arithmetic	Kopfrechnen
distinguish (to, r)	unterscheiden
abbreviation	Abkürzung
seldom	selten

Exercise

And now it is your turn. How would an Englishman say the following times?

18.20 = The time is 20 minutes past 6.	11.55 =
11.00 = The time is	18.29 =
19.45 =	19.31 =
08.15 =	00.05 =
13.00 =	12.00 =
10.30 =	07.44 =

2.3 The seven days of the week and the twelve months of the year

A year has four seasons which are called: spring, summer, autumn and winter.
The year has twelve months:

January	*April*	*July*	*October*
February	*May*	*August*	*November*
March	*June*	*September*	*December*

A year is usually divided into four quarters:
1st quarter   2nd quarter   3rd quarter   4th quarter
A month usually has four weeks, and a week has seven days. These seven days of the week are called:

Monday Tuesday Wednesday Thursday Friday Saturday Sunday

There are five daytimes: morning noon afternoon evening night

Note
The names of the months of the year and of the days of the week must always be written with capital letters!

How to say the year in a date properly

For years up to 1999, the system is easy. You simply split the year into two parts and then use cardinal numbers to say it.
Example: 1998 We say: nineteen-ninety-eight
1919 We say: nineteen-nineteen
Don't forget to put a stress on the ending "...teen" when you say numbers between 13 and 19. Otherwise, these numbers could be easily get confused with 30, 40, 50 etc.. This is especially the case when you make phone calls. So it is best to say:
thirteen – fourteen – fifteen – sixteen – seventeen – eighteen – nineteen
The year 2000 is simply "two thousand". From then on we say "two thousand-one", "two thousand-two" and so on.

Exercise

Now it is your turn. How would you say these dates?
Mo., 14.06.1997 = It is Monday, the fourteenth of June, nineteen-ninety-seven.
Di., 21.07.2008 = It is
Mi., 2.12.2007 =
Do., 31.12.2008 =
Fr., 13.02.2009 =
Sa., 23.09.2002 =

2.4 Public holidays

Public holidays are days when all shops are closed and when nobody (with some exceptions such as the fire brigade, the police, the personnel working for public transport, personnel in hospitals etc.) do not have to work. It is a day off. The typical public holiday is Sunday. But there are other public holidays, too. Here they are:

Public holidays in Germany

	German designation	English designation
01.01.	Neujahr	New Year/New Year's Day
no fixed date	Karfreitag	Good Friday
no fixed date	Ostersonntag	Easter Sunday
no fixed date	Ostermontag	Easter Monday
01.05.	Maifeiertag/Tag der Arbeit	Labour Day
no fixed date	Himmelfahrt	Ascension Day
no fixed date	Pfingstsonntag	Whitsun Sunday
no fixed date	Pfingstmontag	Whitsun Monday
03.10.	Tag der Deutschen Einheit	Reunification Day
24.12.	(Heiligabend)	Christmas Eve
25.12.	1. Weihnachtstag	Christmas Day
26.12.	2. Weihnachtstag	Boxing Day
31.12.	(Silvester)	New Year's Eve

Note

The names of all public holidays must always be written with capital letters!

The two German words for Christmas Eve and New Year's Eve are in brackets because these two days are not official public holidays in Germany, but many people do not work on these two days. In Britain, these two days are of no importance at all, they are normal working days, i.e. people work until 5 o'clock in the late afternoon.

Public holidays in the United Kingdom

01.01.	New Year/New Year's Day
no fixed date	Good Friday
no fixed date	Easter Sunday
no fixed date	Easter Monday
01.05.	Labour Day
no fixed date	Ascension Day
no fixed date	Whitsun Sunday
25.12.	Christmas Day
26.12.	Boxing Day

In addition to the above mentioned public holidays, the British have some extra holidays. Such an extra holiday is called a "bank holiday". It is an official public holiday (on a day other than Saturday and Sunday) when all banks and post offices are closed, as well as most factories, offices and shops. At present the following days are bank holidays in England and Wales:

first Monday in May	May Day bank holiday
last Monday in May	spring bank holiday
last Monday in August	August bank holiday

There is a very interesting regulation for public holidays such as Christmas Day, Boxing Day and New Year's Day. If one of these days falls on a Saturday or Sunday, then the next working day (usually the Monday) after this day will be a bank holiday.

Here is an example: Christmas Day is on a Saturday. That means that the British will have Monday and Tuesday off, as well, because these days automatically become bank holidays. In this particular case, the Monday after New Year's Day will also be a bank holiday. So the British are very lucky indeed!

Vocabulary List

public transport	Öffentliche Verkehrmittel
designation	Bezeichnung
fire brigade	Feuerwehr
above mentioned	oben erwähnt, vorher beschrieben
in brackets	in Klammern
factory	Fabrik
to have a day off	einen Tag frei haben
become (to, ir)	werden
particular	speziell, besonders

Section 3 Brush up your grammar

3.1 The personal pronouns *Die persönlichen Fürwörter*

In der englischen Sprache gibt es genauso viele persönliche Fürwörter wie in der deutschen Sprache. Es sind insgesamt acht:

English		German	deutsche Bezeichnung
I	=	*ich*	*1. Person Einzahl*
you	=	*du*	*2. Person Einzahl*
he	=	*er*	*3. Person Einzahl männlich*
she	=	*sie*	*3. Person Einzahl weiblich*
it	=	*es*	*3. Person Einzahl sächlich*
we	=	*wir*	*1. Person Mehrzahl*
you	=	*ihr*	*2. Person Mehrzahl*
they	=	*sie*	*3. Person Mehrzahl*

The possessive pronouns *Die besitzanzeigenden Fürwörter*

Adjektivisch (vor dem Nomen)
I have lost my money. ... *mein Geld*
You have lost your money. ... *dein Geld*
He has lost his money. ... *sein Geld*
She has lost her money. ... *ihr Geld*
It has lost its money. ... *sein Geld*
We have lost our money. ... *unser Geld*
You have lost your money. ... *euer Geld*
They have lost their money. ... *ihr Geld*

substantivisch (alleinstehend)
This book is mine. ... *meins*
This book is yours. ... *deins*
This book is his. ... *seins*
This book is hers. ... *ihrs*
This book is its. ... *seins*
These books are ours. ... *unseres*
These books are yours. ... *eures*
These books are theirs. ... *ihres*

Rückbezüglich
I help myself.
You help yourself.
He helps himself.
She helps herself.
It helps itself.
We help ourselves.
You help yourselves.
They help themselves.

3.2 The verbs *Die Verben*

In der englischen Sprache haben wir zwei verschiedene Arten von Verben. Wir nennen sie "regelmäßige Verben" (regular verbs) und "unregelmäßige Verben" (irregular verbs). Die Anwendung der regelmäßigen Verben ist einfach. Wir setzen einfach die Endung "-ed" hinter die Grundform des Verbs, wenn wir die Zeiten "Vergangenheit" (simple past tense) oder die vollendete Gegenwart/vollendete Vergangenheit (present perfect/past perfect tense) bilden wollen. Hier ist ein Beispiel für ein regelmäßiges Verb:

To work	= arbeiten		
arbeiten	= work	= present tense	(Gegenwart)
arbeitete	= worked	= simple past tense	(Vergangenheit)
habe gearbeitet	= have worked	= present perfect tense	(vollendete Gegenwart)

Bei den unregelmäßigen Verben ist es etwas schwieriger. Wie der Name schon sagt, sind diese Verben unregelmäßig, und das heißt, dass die Zeiten „simple past tense“ und „present perfect/past perfect“nicht auf die regelmäßige Weise durch Anhängen von „-ed“ an die Grundform des Verbs gebildet werden. Hier ist ein Beispiel für ein unregelmäßiges Verb:

to take	= nehmen		
nehmen	= take	= present tense	(Gegenwart)
nahm	= took	= simple past tense	(Vergangenheit)
habe genommen	= have taken	= present perfect tense	(vollendete Gegenwart)

Im Anhang dieses Buches befindet sich eine Liste, die alle wichtigen unregelmäßigen Verben enthält. Besser jedoch, als einzelne Verben nachzuschlagen ist es, diese Liste zu lernen, um im Umgang mit der englischen Sprache diese Verben zu kennen.

3.3 The tenses *Die Zeiten*

The present tense *Die Gegenwart*

Genau wie in der deutschen Sprache gibt es auch in der englischen Sprache eine ganze Reihe von Zeiten, aber die wichtigsten im Umgang mit der englischen Sprache sind: Gegenwart (present), Vergangenheit (simple past) und Zukunft („will“-future).
Die Zeit „Gegenwart“ (present) verwenden wir immer dann, wenn wir eine Handlung beschreiben, die jetzt im Moment stattfindet. Die Bildung der Zeit „Gegenwart“ (present)

ist einfach, allerdings muss man hier darauf achten, dass man den Buchstaben „s“ bei der dritten Person Einzahl (he, she, it) an das Verb anhängt.
Hier ist ein Beispiel für die Verwendung eines regelmäßigen Verbs in der Gegenwart:
to work = arbeiten
I work
you work
he works
she works
it works
we work
you work
they work

Note

Nicht vergessen: "he, she, it" – das "s" muss mit!

Diese Regel gilt nur in der Zeit "present", bei den anderen Zeiten wie "simple past", "present perfect" etc. gilt sie nicht. Da ist die Form des bei allen Personen gleich.

The simple past tense *Die einfache Vergangenheit*

Man verwendet die Zeit einfache Vergangenheit (simple past) für alle Handlungen, die schon vor einiger Zeit stattgefunden haben, das heißt in der Vergangenheit. Wie schon vorher erwähnt, gibt es zwei verschiedene Arten von Verben, nämlich regelmäßige und unregelmäßige Verben.
Bei regelmäßigen Verben fügt man in der Vergangenheit einfach die Endung "-ed" an die Grundform des Verbs an. Hier ist ein Beispiel:
to work = arbeiten Die Vergangenheitsform für dieses Verb lautet "worked".
I worked
you worked
he worked
she worked
it worked
we worked
you worked
they worked
Bei unregelmäßigen Verben muss man die entsprechende Form des Verbs verwenden, die in der Liste im Anhang dieses Buches zu finden sind. Hier ist ein Beispiel dafür:
to go = gehen Die Vergangenheitform dieses Verbs ist: "went"
I went
you went
he went
she went
it went
we went
you went
they went

The future

Die Zukunft

Die Bildung der Zeit Zukunft in der englischen Sprache ist sehr einfach, denn es gibt hier keine Unregelmäßigkeiten. Zur Bildung des „future“ brauchen wir das Modalverb „will“ und das Verb in seiner Grundform.

Beispiel:	I will go	ich werde gehen
	you will go	du wirst gehen
	he will go	er wird gehen
	she will go	sie wird gehen
	it will go	es wird gehen
	we will go	wir werden gehen
	you will go	ihr werdet gehen
	they will go	sie werden gehen

3.4 Capital letters or not?

Großschreibung oder nicht?

Häufig ist es recht schwierig zu entscheiden, ob ein englisches Wort mit einem Großbuchstaben geschrieben wird oder ob es kleingeschrieben werden muss. Es gibt aber eine Regel, die bei dieser Entscheidung helfen kann. Mithilfe unserer Hand kann diese Regel eingesetzt werden. Die Hand hat fünf Finger, und genauso viele Dinge wie die Hand Finger hat werden in der englischen Sprache am Wortanfang groß geschrieben. Dazu gehören natürlich auch noch das Wort „I“ (für „ich“) und der Satzanfang, die immer mit einem Großbuchstaben beginnen müssen. Die fünf Finger der Hand bedeuten:

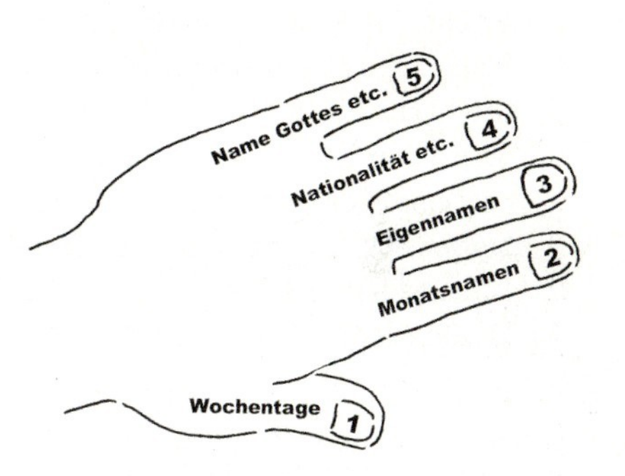

- *der Daumen* = *Er steht für die Wochentage.*
  the thumb = It stands for the days of the week.
- *der Zeigefinger* = *Er steht für die Namen der 12 Monate des Jahres.*
  the index finger = It stands for the names of the twelve months of the year.
- *der Mittelfinger* = *Er steht für Eigennamen, Vornamen, Städtenamen usw.*
  the middle finger = It stands for proper names, surnames, names of towns etc.
- *der Ringfinger* = *Er steht für Ländernamen, Nationalitäten, Sprachen usw.*
  the ring finger = It stands for nations, nationalities, languages.
- *der kleine Finger* = *Er steht für den Namen Gottes und dazugehörige Begriffe.*
  the little finger = It stands for the name of God and related words.

Vocabulary List

capital letter	Großbuchstabe
thumb	Daumen
proper name	Eigenname
regular verb	regelmäßiges Verb
irregular verb	unregelmäßiges Verb
appropriate	entsprechend
sentence	Satz

Exercise

Translation

Please translate the following sentences from German to English:

1 Heute stellen wir Michael Crocker vor, er ist 19 Jahre alt.
2 Michael Crocker wohnt in einer kleinen Stadt in Niedersachsen.
3 Er hat eine Stelle als Verkäufer in einem großen Supermarkt.
4 Seine Schwestern sind in einem Internat in England.
5 Michael muss oft spät arbeiten.
6 Sein Vater hat ein neues Auto, er parkt es vor dem Haus.
7 Seine Mutter spricht Deutsch und Englisch fließend.
8 Seine Großeltern wohnen in derselben Stadt.
9 Michael hat viele Fragen über London.
10 Heute darf Michael seine Arbeit sehr früh beenden, denn er hat Frühschicht.

Section 4 Practice your word power

4.1 Exercise Word groups

Put each of the words below into the correct list. *Use each word only once!*
Can you think of more words to add to each list?

Squash manager time walls rain cap
cashier shirt snow minute doors cricket
jacket windows tennis floor dial coat
clouds pullover cleaner basketball wind hands
entrance hour assistant rugby hail apprentice
second ceiling trousers sunshine football assistant manageress

1 The clock

....
....
....
....
....
....

2 The building (the supermarket)

....
....
....
....
....
....

3 Clothing

....
....
....
....
....
....

4 Jobs in a supermarket

....
....
....
....
....
....

5 The weather

....
....
....
....
....
....

6 Sports

....
....
....
....
....
....

4.2 Exercise Odd man out

Only one answer is right. Which one is it?

1 One of these is not food. Which one is it?
   a honey b jam c coke
   d ham e spam
2 Beef is meat from a
   a sheep b pig c horse
   d cow e rabbit
3 One of these is not red. Which one is it?
   a cherry b rose c strawberry
   d butter e raspberry

4 Wine is made from
a pears b grapes c grapefruit
d plums e gooseberries

5 One of these is not part of a computer system. Which one is it?
a mouse b monitor c chips
d printer e crisps

6 One of these is not a vegetable. Which one is it?
a Brussels sprouts b cauliflower c pear
d peas e beans

7 One of these is not a drink. Which one is it?
a Coke b wine c milk
d beer e coke

8 Marmalade is a sweet breadspread made of
a plums b melons c strawberries
d oranges e kiwis

9 One of these has nothing to do with milk. Which one is it?
a cow b grass c dairy
d bucket e bee

10 The favourite drink of the British is
a tea with lemon b tea with sugar c black coffee
d coffee with milk e tea with milk and sugar

11 One of these does not grow on a tree. Which one is it?
a plum b pumpkin c lemon
d orange e coconut

12 The salary is the money you get for your work. How often is it paid?
a once a week
b every day
c every two weeks
d once a month
e every three months

13 Which of these is not brown?
A chocolate b coconut c potato
d leaves in autumn e cream

14 The part of the room above your head is the
a ceiling b wall c floor
d door e window

15 One of these is not made from potatoes. Which one is it?
a crisps b chips c mash
d ham e vodka

16 Where do you have to go if you want to buy some black pudding?
a cheese counter b florist c baker
d butcher e grocer

17 One of these is never eaten raw. Which one is it?
a tomato b potato c cherry
d melon e redcurrant

18 Banknotes and coins are also called
a cash b dash c wash
d posh e nosh

19 One of these is different from the others. Which one is it?
   a water   b rain   c wine
   d milk   e bones
20 Now you have a toothache from eating all these sweet things. Who will help you?
   a butcher   b dentist   c undertaker
   d cashier   e priest

4.3 Exercise Definitions

half an hour   Boxing Day   hamburger   water   food
teacher   immediately   fruits   milk   summer
floor   midnight   Friday   night   snow
Wednesday   hands   grandfather   Berlin   supermarket

1 Things we can eat are usually called
2 This white liquid comes from a cow, butter and cheese are made of it
3 the hottest of the four seasons of the year
4 the third working day after Sunday
5 12.00 p.m.
6 Thirty minutes are
7 Frozen rain is called
8 The second day after Christmas Eve is
9 The two parts of a clock which show us the time on the dial are the
10 A slice of minced beef between the two halves of a spongy roll is called a
11 The period of time between 12.00 p.m. and 06.00 a.m. is the
12 To wash your hands, you need soap and
13 The person who helps you to learn English is your
14 The part of the room underneath your feet is the
15 Strawberries, plums and apples are
16 The capital of Germany is
17 Your father's father is your
18 Another word for "at once" is
19 A big shop where you can buy many different things is a
20 The second day before Sunday is

4.4 Exercise Fill the gaps

A very difficult decision

This .... *(Nachmittag)* Michael is allowed to finish work .... *(früh)* .... *(weil)* he is on the .... *(Frühschicht)*

shift this week. He started work at half past six in the morning, the supermarket he works in .... (*normalerweise*) opens at seven o'clock.
Oh sorry, we forgot to .... (*vorstellen*) Michael.
His full name is Michael Crocker, he is 17 years old and he lives in a small town in Lower Saxony in the north of Germany. Michael .... (*wohnen*) with his parents. They have a house near the army barracks. Michael's father Gordon is an officer in the British army. His mother Renate is German, so Michael grew up bilingual, that means that he can .... (*sprechen*) English and German fluently. Michael also has two younger sisters named Sharon and Jennifer, but they are not at home with the family, they are in a .... (*Internat*) in England. Michael, however, went to school in Germany. He finished school last year at the age of 16 and then found a job as an assistant in the local "SUPRA"-supermarket, a .... (*Kette*) of supermarkets for the British Forces in Germany. He loves to work there .... (*weil*) he likes to work with people, and he finds working with .... (*Kunden*) very interesting. The supermarket he works for is for the British Forces, but Michael absolves a proper .... (*Lehre*) under German regulations, and once a week he has to go to the local "Berufsschule" – the vocational training college.
When Michael comes home this .... (*Nachmittag*) shortly after three o'clock, he sees his father's car parked in front of the house. So his dad is already home. This is unusual .... (*weil*) his father often has to work late, and sometimes he is away for a long time .... (*weil*) he is on exercise. Michael immediately sees that .... (*etwas*) unusual must have happened .... (*weil*) his father has a .... (*Brief*) in his hand which looks very official. What could it be? Now his father tells him that he will have to go back to England, the army has posted him wef 1st of June to a garrison in the south of England, not too far away from London. This is a shock for Michael. He has just begun his training, what would .... (*geschehen*) him? Would he have to go to England .... (*zusammen*) with his parents? Would it be better for him to stay in Germany and finish his .... (*Lehre*) first? Of course, he could stay with his grandparents (his mother's parents) who live in the same town. But what about all his friends in town and at work? But on the other hand, London is luring! So many .... (*Fragen*)! All evening, the family sits .... (*zusammen*) and discusses the .... (*Zukunft*).

Section 1 Texts

Text 1 The first step is always the hardest

Our friend Michael spent some very exciting weeks. Remember, he lived with his family in Germany. His father is British, he is in the British army, and his mother is German. Some weeks ago, his father got posted to England to a small town near London. The Crockers now live in a very nice semi-detached house in the outskirts of the town. With the help of his store manager in Germany, Michael found a new job in the U.K. right away. He will now work in a TESCO supermarket not far away from the house they now live in. Today (it's Monday.) is his first working day, so Michael got up very early. He wanted to be there in time.

After breakfast (it was a typical English breakfast with cornflakes, bacon, baked beans, sausages and fried eggs and, of course, toast and marmalade and plenty of tea with milk and sugar) he took his mountain bike and rode to the local supermarket. A friendly-looking man in a white coat stood at the staff entrance of the market. Obviously he was waiting for Michael.

Michael locked his bike on a chain and walked over to the man in the white coat. "Good morning, sir. I suppose you are the store manager and you are waiting for me. Is that right?"

The name of the store manager is Mr Willy Wellwood, and he now gave Michael a very friendly welcome: "Good morning, Michael. You are right, I have been waiting for you, but only a few minutes. I am glad to see that you arrived on time. My name is Willy Wellwood, I am the store manager. Please come with me to my office." They walked all the way through the entrance area of the market to the store manager's office where a young lady was already waiting for them. Mr Wellwood now introduced Michael to Sharon Robinson, the assistant manageress of the supermarket. She smiled and stretched out her hand. "How do you do, Michael?" she asked. Michael knew quite well what the only possible answer to this question during a formal introduction was. Therefore, he took Sharon's hand, shook it and answered: "How do you do, Miss Robinson?" Sharon smiled at him again and asked him to simply call her Sharon. Now Mr Wellwood turned to Michael again: "All right, Michael, after you have been issued with a proper working dress, Sharon will show you the market this morning. You will see that it is quite big, all in all we run 25 departments or sections. Sharon will then make a shift roster for you. Remember, in this supermarket we have to work shift because of our opening hours. All our staff have every other weekend off, and so will you. Furthermore, Sharon will take the necessary details for your personal file which we have to send to London. We also need a health certificate for you, so we have already arranged for an appointment with a physician. You will see Dr Feelgood (he is responsible for health matters) tomorrow morning for a health check. Sharon will tell you when you have to be there and where his surgery is. And now, Michael, go ahead and look!" After the introduction, Sharon asked him to follow her, and so they left the manager's office for a tour round the market. Michael was deeply impressed. This supermarket was so much bigger than the one he worked for in Germany. Some things were different from German supermarkets. There was, for example, a very big sandwich bar in the entrance zone or lobby where people could rush in and buy some sandwiches for lunch or tea without having to wait very long at the normal checkouts. This place was crowded. One after the other, they visited all the different departments of the market, and all the time, Sharon gave him much information. She also told him that he should explore the market by himself again tomorrow afternoon in order to really familiarize himself with it. Before he knocked off, Sharon told him that he would have to work in the greengrocery department tomorrow morning. This week, he was on the morning shift, so he had to be at work fairly early.

Vocabulary List

spend (to, ir)	Zeit verbringen; auch: Geld ausgeben
semi-detached house	Doppelhaushälfte
outskirts (the)	Stadtrand
ride (to, ir)	reiten; hier: Fahrrad fahren
coat	Mantel; hier: Kittel
obviously	offensichtlich
suppose (to, r)	annehmen, vermuten
on time	pünktlich
introduce (to, r)	vorstellen, einführen
issue (to, r)	ausgeben
shift	Arbeitsschicht
shift roster	Schichtplan, Dienstplan
every other weekend	jedes zweite Wochenende
health certificate	Gesundheitszeugnis
appointment	Termin; hier: Arzttermin
physician	prakt. Arzt, Allgemeinmediziner
surgery	Arztpraxis
crowded	überfüllt durch viele Menschen
explore (to, r)	erkunden
familiarize (to, r)	vertraut machen
knock off (to)	Feierabend machen

For the irregular verbs in this story which are all in the past tense please refer to the "ABC of irregular verbs" in the annex of this book.

Text 2 New impressions galore

The morning shift always has to begin early, everything in the market has to be ready before the first customers arrive. That is why Michael only ate a quick breakfast (a slice of toast and a glass of milk) this morning. He did not have the time to wait for the rest of the family. After he had arrived at the market, he reported to the shift supervisor on the ramp. A lorry with fresh vegetables and fruits had just arrived, it had to be unloaded, and the crates had

to be taken to the storeroom. From there, the vegetables were taken to the appropriate department where they were nicely arranged on shelves and gondolas. Another lorry
15 arrived. The driver reported to the ramp supervisor (the person responsible for unloading), and then the supervisor told Michael and two of his colleagues to unload this vehicle, too. The strawberry season had just begun, and that was why large quantities of fresh strawberries had to be unloaded and put into cool storage. The strawberries were all in plastic trays which contained one pound of fruits, and the berries were covered with a thin plastic film
20 to keep them fresh and protected. And there were lots of other things that arrived this morning: crates filled with cauliflowers, lettuce and leeks, sacks with potatoes and onions and many other vegetables.
Michael finished this job at the ramp at 9 o'clock. Now he had two hours time to make himself familiar with the market and all its departments, so he walked around and looked
25 at everything. He was quite impressed to see the big shelves filled with all sorts of items, the large cold shelves in the departments for dairy products and meat and the long freezers in the frozen food department. Everything here was much bigger than in the supermarket back in Germany where he began to learn his trade. And he noticed something else: Cleanliness was of utmost importance in all the TESCO supermarkets. Whenever some-
30 thing fell down on the floor and soiled it, it was removed straight away.
During his lunch break (sandwiches from the sandwich bar, of course), Michael had the chance to talk to some other young people who work with him. It turned out that one of the boys, his name is Pete, lived not too far from Michael's home. His father is in the army, too. Pete currently worked in the drinks department. He did not like that job too much
35 because full crates with bottles in them are quite heavy, and lots of these had to be handled and stacked every day. But Pete also understood quite well that the job had to be done, so he did not complain or moan.
In the afternoon after his lunch break, Michael had to accompany one of his colleagues. Their task now was to check the shelves in the grocery department, they had to look for
40 items that were in low supply. For this job, they used a portable electronic scanner not much bigger than a mobile phone. All they had to do was to read the bar code in front of the shelf, the scanner then told them how many items were left and how many they should have in stock. To order new supplies, they simply had to press a button on the scanner, the rest was done by the computer in the admin office.

Vocabulary List

impression	Eindruck
galore	in Hülle und Fülle
shift supervisior	Schichtführer
lorry	Lastwagen
appropriate	entsprechend
quantity	Menge
cleanliness	Sauberkeit
utmost	allerhöchst
soil (to, r)	verschmutzen
remove (to, r)	entfernen

complain (to, r)	beschweren
moan (to, r)	beklagen
accompany (to, r)	begleiten
bar code	Strichcode
in stock	am Lager
Supply	Versorgung, Nachschub, Nachlieferung

For the irregular verbs in this story which are all in the past tense please refer to the "ABC of irregular verbs" in the annex of this book.

Comprehension exercise

Please answer the following questions in full sentences.

1 What did Michael do on his first working day before he went to work?
2 What happened in the manager's office?
3 What exactly does it mean when you have to work shift?
4 Why does Michael have to see the doctor?
5 Where will Michael have to start work the morning after his first day?
6 What kind of work did he have to do at the ramp?
7 How did Michael familiarize himself with his new workplace?
8 Why did Michael's friend Pete not like his job in the drinks department too much?
9 How is the existing stock in a modern supermarket checked?
10 How are new supplies ordered in a modern supermarket?

Section 2 Basics The supermarket

2.1 The basic building

The basic components of a building are:

- the floor — der Fußboden
- the walls — die Wände
- the ceiling — die Decke
- the roof — das Dach
- the windows — die Fenster
- the doors — die Türen
- the rooms — die Zimmer/Räume
- the storeys — die Etagen/Stockwerke
- the corridors — die Flure/Korridore

The furniture and the equipment (general):

- table — Tisch
- desk — Schreibtisch
- chair — Stuhl
- stool — Hocker

- locker Schrank
- sideboard Anrichte
- lamp Lampe
- fire extinguisher Feuerlöscher
- ladder Leiter
- stepladder Trittleiter
- dustbin Abfalleimer
- basin Waschbecken
- tap Wasserhahn

The furniture and the special equipment of a supermarket:

- counter Tresen
- shelf Regal
- cold shelf Kühltruhe
- freezer Gefriertruhe
- fridge Kühlschrank
- gondola Verkaufstisch
- cash register Registrierkasse
- scanner Lesegerät
- conveyor belt Laufband
- trolley Einkaufswagen
- basket Einkaufskorb

2.2 The departments of a supermarket

- grocery allgemeine Lebensmittel
- greengrocery Obst und Gemüse
- butchery/fresh meat Fleischerei
- dairy products Milchprodukte
- fish & seafood Fisch und Meeresfrüchte
- tinned food Konserven
- herbs & spices Kräuter und Gewürze
- delicatessen Delikatessen
- exotic food ausländische Lebensmittel
- confectionery Süßwaren
- frozen food Tiefkühlkost
- convenience food Fertiggerichte
- drinks Getränke
- household products Haushalts- und Reinigungsmittel
- toiletries Hygieneartikel
- chemistry Drogerieartikel
- cosmetics Kosmetikartikel
- stationery Büroartikel
- household utensils Haushaltswaren
- pet food Tiernahrung
- haberdashery Kurzwaren

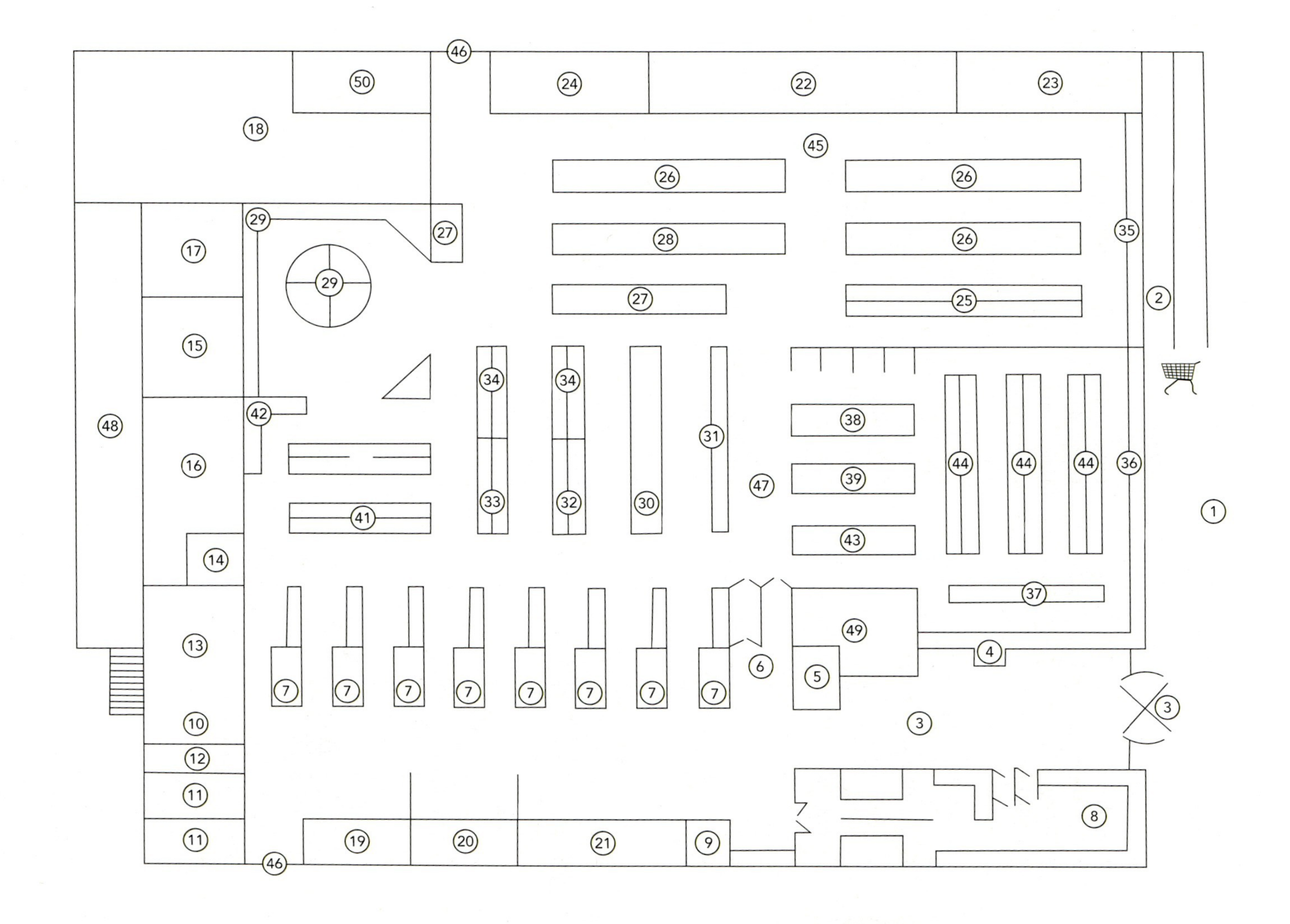
1
2
3
4
5
6
7
8
9
10
11
12
13
14
15
16
17
18
19
20
21
22
23
24
25
26
27
28
29
30
31
32
33
34
35
36
37
38
39
41
42
43
44
45
46
47
48
49
50

2.3 Market guide

	English	German
1	car park	Parkplatz
2	trolleys	Einkaufswagen
3	shop entrance/lobby	Eingang
4	ATM	Geldautomat
5	information desk	Information
6	barriers	Schranken Eingangsbereich
7	checkout	Kasse
8	sandwich bar	Sandwichverkauf
9	resting area/benches	Ruhebereich mit Sitzbänken
10	baby care	Babywickelraum
11	toilets (ladies & gents)	Toiletten (Damen und Herren)
12	toilet for the handicapped	Behindertentoilette
13	store manager's office	Büro Marktleiter
14	checkout supervisor's office	Büro Kassenaufsicht
15	social rooms market staff	Sozialräume für Personal
16	market admin office	Büro der Marktverwaltung
17	food preparation area	Zubereitungsraum
18	storeroom	Lagerraum
19	florist	Blumenhändler
20	bakery	Bäckerei
21	hot snacks/cafeteria	Schnellimbiss
22	fresh meat counter	Fleischtheke
23	cheese and deli counter	Käsetheke
24	fish and seafood	Fisch und Meeresfrüchte
25	dairy products	Milchprodukte
26	frozen food	Tiefkühlkost
27	ice cream	Speiseeis
28	convenience food	Fertiggerichte
29	fruit & vegetables	Obst und Gemüse
30	grocery	Lebensmittel
31	herbs & spices	Kräuter und Gewürze
32	tinned food	Konserven
33	confectionery	Süßwaren
34	exotic food	ausländische Feinkost
35	bread & cake/biscuits	Backwaren
36	drinks (soft drinks, beer and wine, spirits)	Getränke
37	bar snacks	Knabbereien (Erdnüsse, Chips etc
38	chemistry/toiletries/ household products	Drogerieabteilung
39	baby food/baby products	Babynahrung/Babypflege
40	pet food	Tiernahrung
41	newspapers and magazines, greetings cards	Zeitungen/Zeitschriften/Glückwunschkarten

	English	Deutsch
42	CDs and DVDs	CDs und DVDs
43	stationery	Schreibwaren
44	household utensils	Haushaltsartikel
45	ticket dispenser	Nummernausgabegerät
46	emergency exit	Notausgang
47	aisle	Gang zwischen den Regalen
48	ramp/unloading area	Rampe/Entladezone
49	children's playroom	Spielzimmer
50	frozen food storage	Tiefkühl-Lagerraum

2.4 Manners – never out of fashion

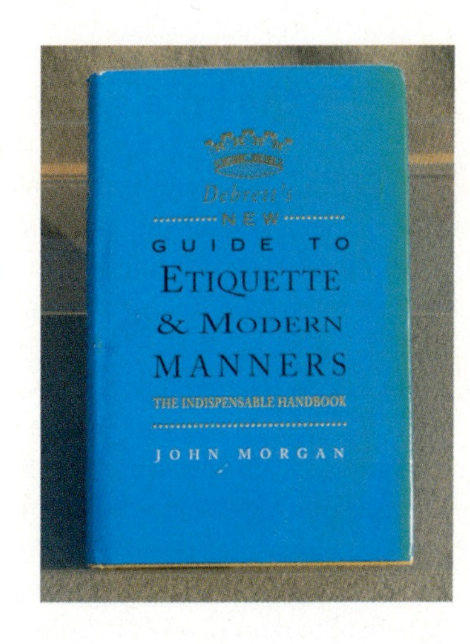

An important factor – not only when you apply for a job but especially when you do business with customers or when you meet the parents of your boyfriend or girlfriend for the first time – is the impression you leave. Luckily there are certain rules which you will have to follow.

- Manners are helpful rules which you can follow if you are not certain what to do or what to say.
- Manners make contacts with other people a lot easier.
- Manners simply make everyday life more friendly and just nicer.
- Manners will make sure that the interviewer gets a good impression of the applicant.

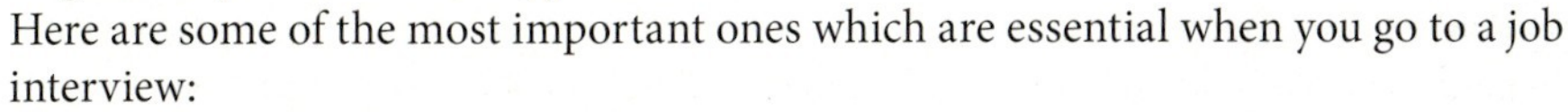

Here are some of the most important ones which are essential when you go to a job interview:

- Turn up in time for your interview, or, even better, five minutes before the time they gave you in their letter of invitation.
- Keep your fingernails short and clean.
- Don't forget to take off your cap when you enter a room.
- Make sure you wear decent and clean clothing, you must not be
- "dressed to kill" when you go to a job interview.
- Tattoos and piercings are not very well liked by employers – remove your piercings before you go to a job interview, keep tattoos covered by your clothing.
- Leave your MP3-player/CD-player and other electronic devices at home.
- Switch your mobile phone off before you enter the room. It is even better to leave it at home. Your future employer is not interested in the sounds your phone can make when it rings.
- Always say: "You are welcome" when someone says: "Thank you" to you.
- Never sit down before you are told to do so.
- In Britain the handshake is not as common as it is in Germany. You better wait until the other person reaches his/her hand out for yours. Then you may shake it.
- Always put your hand on your mouth when you have to yawn.

- When somebody in a formal situation introduces you to a person who is older than you, this person often says: "How do you do?" The only possible answer to that is: "How do you do?". Never say anything else!
- Customers older than yourself are to be addressed as "Madam" in case it is a lady and as "Sir" in case it is a man
- Never ever interrupt anybody. Wait until the person has finished.
- Always bear in mind that it is bad manners to say just "Yes" or "No". You must always add a so-called tag to your answer, so you should (for example) say
- "Yes, it is", "Yes, I am", "Yes, I have" etc. and "No, it isn't", "No, I am not", "No, I haven't" etc.

2.5 On the little word "must" *Über das kleine Wort "must"*

Beim Gebrauch des englischen Wortes "must" ist große Vorsicht geboten. Dieses Wort hat nicht dieselbe Bedeutung wie das deutsche Wort „müssen". Wir Deutschen verwenden das Wort "müssen" recht unbefangen. So sagen wir durchaus zu einem Kunden „Dann müssen Sie dort im dritten Regal schauen". Im Deutschen ist diese Aussage keineswegs unfreundlich.
In der englischen Sprache dagegen steckt hinter dem Wort "must" immer eine Art Drohung, das heißt, es ist mit Folgen bzw. Konsequenzen zu rechnen, wenn die mit "must" formulierte Aufforderung nicht befolgt wird.
Beispiel: Der Marktleiter fordert einen Angestellten auf "You must come on time" *(Sie müssen pünktlich kommen).*
Tut er das nicht, dann hat er mit arbeitsrechtlichen Folgen zu rechnen.
Daher sollte man das Wort "müssen" in der englischen Sprache besser durch "have to" (Beispiel: "You have to go to the fresh meat counter) ersetzen. Dann fühlt sich der Angesprochene nicht in die Enge getrieben.
Außerdem kann das Wort "must" nur im "present tense" (Gegenwart) verwendet werden, im "simple past" (Vergangenheit) heißt es immer "had to".

Section 3 Brush up your grammar

3.1 Plurals *Die Mehrzahl der Hauptwörter*

Grundregel:

Wir bilden die Mehrzahl der meisten Hauptwörter durch Anhängen des Buchstaben "s".

Beispiele:
one bottle – two bottles
a flower – some flowers
one basket – three baskets

Unregelmäßige Pluralbildung

Irregular plurals

Abhängig von den letzten Buchstaben eines Hauptwortes ist die Pluralbildung unregelmäßig entsprechend der folgenden Regeln:

Nomen mit Endung	Beispiele
-ss -sh -ch -x	glass – glasses brush – brushes church – churches box – boxes
-o	tomato – tomatoes
-io	radio – radios
-y	city – cities
-vowel+y	journey – journeys boy – boys
-f -fe	shelf – shelves wife – wives
-oof	roof – roofs

Es gibt einige Sonderformen(unregelmäßige Mehrzahl), die man auswendig lernen muss:
man – men woman – women child – children mouse – mice louse – lice
tooth – teeth foot – feet goose – geese penny – pence

Folgende Wörter haben keine eigene Mehrzahl, sondern hier ist die Form der Einzahl identisch mit der Form der Mehrzahl.:
fish – fish sheep – sheep salmon – salmon trout – trout

Sonderfälle:
photo – photos (weil es von "photograph" kommt)
piano – pianos (weil es von "piano forte" kommt)

Exercise Plurals

Fill in the correct plural forms of the words.

1 box ____________________
2 foot ____________________
3 head ____________________
4 office ____________________
5 potato ____________________
6 door ____________________
7 manageress ____________________
8 life ____________________
9 reason ____________________
10 message ____________________
11 vacancy ____________________
12 application ____________________
13 enquiry ____________________
14 tomato ____________________
15 brush ____________________
16 fly ____________________

17 fireman	____________	29 play	____________
18 journey	____________	30 house	____________
19 town	____________	31 noodle	____________
20 city	____________	32 day	____________
21 responsibility	____________	33 lorry	____________
22 glass	____________	34 salary	____________
23 tooth	____________	35 brush	____________
24 housewife	____________	36 roof	____________
25 gentleman	____________	37 child	____________
26 country	____________	38 fox	____________
27 shelf	____________	39 dish	____________
28 story	____________	40 policewoman	____________

3.2 The simple present tense with ordinary verbs

Der Satzbau mit Vollverben in der Gegenwart

Beispiele: I get up at 7 o'clock.
Do you get up early?
I do not get up before 7.30.

Es gibt folgende Satzarten:

Aussagesatz	> **statement**
Frage	> **question**
Verneinung	> negation (saying "no".)

Beispiele:

	Aussage	Frage	Verneinung
SINGULAR	I *drink* tea.	*Do* I *drink* tea?	I *do not drink* tea.
	You *drink* tea.	*Do* you *drink* tea?	You *do not drink* tea.
	He *drinks* tea.	*Does* he *drink* tea?	He *does not drink* tea.
	She *drinks* tea.	*Does* she *drink* tea?	She *does not drink* tea.
	It *drinks* tea.	*Does* it *drink* tea?	It *does not drink* tea.
PLURAL	We *drink* tea.	*Do* we *drink* tea?	We *do not drink* tea.
	You *drink* tea.	*Do* you *drink* tea?	You *do not drink* tea.
	They *drink* tea.	*Do* they *drink* tea?	They *do not drink* tea.

Wichtige Regeln:

Aussagen:
Bei der dritten Person Singular muss immer das "s" an das Verb angehängt werden.

Note
Merksatz: "He, she, it" – das "s" muss mit!

Beispiel: Peter drinks tea. >>> He drinks tea.
Die Struktur sieht wie folgt aus: noun/pronoun + verb(+s)

Fragestellung/questions:
Um eine Frage zu bilden, verwendet man "do".Bei "he", "she" or "it" wird "es" an das Verb "do" angehängt.
Das Verb steht in der Grundform (ohne "s").

Beispiele: Do the students learn? Do they learn?
Does Peter drink tea? Does he drink tea?

Die Struktur sieht wie folgt aus: do/does + noun/pronoun + verb (infinitive)

Verneinung/negations:
Um einen Aussagesatz zu verneinen verwendet man do not (don't) oder in der dritten Person Singular does not (doesn't).

Beispiele: The students do not learn. They do not learn.
Peter does not drink tea. He does not drink tea.

Die Satzstruktur ist dieselbe wie in
Aussagen: noun/pronoun + do/does +not + verb (infinitive)

Bildung: Wann hängt man bei der 3. Person Singular "s" an und wann "es"?

Verben mit Endung -ch, -sh, -s, -x:	Bei Verben mit einem Konsonanten vor dem "y" wird das "y" zu einem "i", und es wird "-es" angehängt:	Sonderformen:
reach – reaches	try – tries	have – has
wash – washes	reply – replies	go – goes
miss – misses		do – does
fix – fixes		

Exercise: The simple present tense with complete verbs
Die Bildung der einfachen Vergangenheit mit Vollverben

Beispiel: Michael (to live) in a big town. (small town)

Aussage (s): Michael lives in a big town.
Frage (q): Does Michael live in a small town?
Verneinung (n): Michael does not live in a small town.

Form sentences, questions and negations as shown in the example. Use the "simple present tense".

1 Michael's mother (to work) as a correspondent. (waitress)
2 They (to live) in a terraced house. (block of flats)
3 His cousins Ian and Brian (to go) to school. (a disco)
4 Sharon (to see) her boyfriend Stevie twice a week. (every day)
5 Mr Wellwood sometimes (to drive) the company car. (a bus)
6 He (to have) a driving licence. (his own car)
7 Mrs Hesketh (to care) for young children while their parents are shopping. (the dogs)
8 Michael and Carrie-Ann (to dance) on Saturdays. (Wednesdays)
9 Dinah (to leave) school in summer. (in spring)
10 Michael (to start) work at seven o'clock in the morning. (evening)

3.3 Comparison of adjectives

Das Steigern der Eigenschaftswörter

Grundregel I/basic rule I: Short adjectives

An kurze Adjektive (1 oder 2 Silben) hängt man –er und –est an.
e.g. long – longer – the longest, clever – cleverer – the cleverest

Adjektive, die auf –y enden, verwandeln das y in ein i.
e.g. happy – happier – the happiest

Kurze Adjektive mit nur einem Vokal verdoppeln den Endkonsonanten.
e.g. fat – fatter – the fattest, big – bigger – the biggest

An kurze Adjektive, die auf –e enden, hängt man nur noch –r und –st an.
e.g. nice – nicer – the nicest

Grundregel II/basic rule II: Longer adjectives

Adjektive, die mehr als zwei Silben haben, steigert man mit "more" und "most".

e.g. wonderful – more wonderful – the most wonderful
intelligent – more intelligent – the most intelligent

Zusatzregel:

Alle Adjektive, die auf –id oder –ous enden, werden immer mit "more" und "most" gesteigert, auch wenn sie kurz sind.

e.g. stupid – more stupid – the most stupid
famous – more famous – the most famous

Grundregel III/basic rule III: Irregular comparison

Einige Adjektive haben unregelmäßige Formen.

good – better – the best
bad – worse – the worst
much/many – more – the most
little – less – the least

EXERCISE

Bitte steigern Sie die folgenden Adjektive entsprechend den vorher erläuterten Regeln.

1	warm	warmer	the warmest
2	curious	more curious	the most curious
3	important	______	______
4	big	______	______
5	short	______	______
6	difficult	______	______
7	easy	______	______
8	good	______	______
9	dark	______	______
10	beautiful	______	______
11	cheap	______	______
12	little	______	______
13	expensive		

14 rapid ____________ ____________

15 heavy ____________ ____________

16 solid ____________ ____________

17 bad ____________ ____________

18 slim ____________ ____________

19 busy ____________ ____________

Exercise:

3.4 Translate

1 Unser Freund Michael verbrachte einige sehr aufregende Wochen in Deutschland.
2 Seine Eltern wohnen in einer sehr schönen Doppelhaushälfte am Stadtrand.
3 Der Marktleiter begrüßte Michael auf sehr freundliche Weise.
4 Die stellvertretende Marktleiterin stellte einen Dienstplan für Michael auf.
5 In diesem Supermarkt gibt es eine sehr große Sandwich-Bar im Eingangsbereich.
6 Nachdem er im Markt angekommen war, meldete sich Michael beim Schichtführer.
7 Die Erdbeeren waren alle in Kunststoffschalen, jede Schale enthielt ein Pfund.
8 Sauberkeit ist in allen Supermärkten überaus wichtig.
9 Die Arbeit in der Getränkeabteilung ist nicht einfach, denn die Getränkekästen sind schwer.
10 Um neue Waren zu bestellen, muss man einfach den Knopf am Scanner drücken.

Section 4 Practise your word power

4.1 Exercise Word groups

Put each of the words below into the correct list.
Can you think of more words to add to each list?
Use each word only once!

jar ladder walls telephone bakery cashier questions
foil drinks freezer windows microphone cleaner fresh meat
cold shelf tin loudspeaker toilets gondola bottle
sales assistant answers floor box counter doors
frozen food caretaker bag fruits & vegetables shelf
ceiling manager dairy products list of special offers assistant manager

1 The building

....
....
....
....
....
....

2 Furniture/equipment

....
....
....
....
....
....

3 At the information desk

....
....
....
....
....
....

4 Departments of the market

....
....
....
....
....
....

5 The staff

....
....
....
....
....
....

6 Packaging

....
....
....
....
....
....

4.2 Exercise Odd man out

Only one answer is right. Which one is it?

1 One of these is not food. Which one is it?

a ahoney
b jam
c Coke
d biro
e spam

2 Pork is meat from a
a sheep b pig c horse
d cow e rabbit

3 One of these is not black. Which one is it?
a coal b liquorice c blackberry
d night e gooseberry

4 Marmalade is made from
a pears b grapes c grapefruit
d oranges e gooseberries

5 One of these is not part of a computer system. Which one is it?
a rat b monitor c chips
d printer e mouse

6 One of these is not a vegetable. Which one is it?
a cabbage b cauliflower c peas
d pineapple e beans

7 One of these is not a drink. Which one is it?
a tea b wine c milk
d beef e herbal infusion

8 Honey is a sweet breadspread collected by
a bees b ants c butterflies
d flies e bumblebees

9 One of these has nothing to do with beer. Which one is it?
a liquid b brewery c brewer
d hops e sweet

10 The favourite drink of the Americans is
a tea with lemon b tea with sugar c hot black coffee
d coffee with milk e tea with milk and sugar

11 One of these does not grow on a tree. Which one is it?
a cherry b carrot c pear
d orange e walnut

12 The money you get for your work once a month is your

a wages b salary c income tax
d bonus e VAT

13 Which of these is not green?

a cucumber b avocado c potato
d leaves in summer e grass

14 The part of the room below your feet is the

a ceiling b wall c floor
d door e window

15 One of these is not made from flour. Which one is it?

a cake b tart c bread
d biscuit e shandy

16 Where would you have to go if you wanted to buy some chops?

a cheese counter b florist c baker
d butcher e grocer

17 One of these is never cooked. Which one is it?

a tomato b potato c cabbage
d carrot e radish

18 Credit cards are also called

a cash b banknotes c plastic money
d currency e coins

19 One of these is different from the others. Which one is it?

a water b rain c tea
d milk e beer

20 The period of time between 12.00 p.m. and 06.00 a.m. is called

a noon b afternoon c morning
d night e evening

4.3 Exercise Definitions

quarter Christmas Day chop soap drink
manager too vegetables cow winter
lamp noon 2nd of May afternoon ice
Thursday dial grandmother London optician

1 Liquid food is also called
2 The animal milk comes from
3 The coldest of the four seasons of the year
4 The fourth working day after Sunday
5 12.00 a.m.
6 Fifteen minutes are a .... of an hour
7 Frozen water is called
8 The first day after Christmas Eve is
9 The round disc on a clock where the hands show us the time is the
10 A slice of pork or beef with a piece of bone on it is called a
11 The period of time between 12.00 a.m. and 06.00 p.m. is the
12 To wash your hands, you need water and
13 The boss of a supermarket is the
14 The device in a room that gives light
15 Beans, peas and cabbage are
16 The capital of the U.K. is (U.K. = United Kingdom)
17 Your father's mother is your
18 Another word for "also" is
19 A shop where you can buy glasses is an
20 The first day after Labour Day is the

4.4 Exercise Fill the gaps

The first step is always the hardest

Our friend Michael .... *(verbringen)* some very .... *(aufregend)* weeks. Remember, he lived with his family in Germany. His father is British, he is in the British army, and his mother is German. Some weeks ago, his father got posted to England to a small town near London. The Crockers now live in a very nice .... – .... *(Doppelhaushälfte)* in the outskirts of the town. With the help of his store manager in Germany, Michael found a new job in the U.K. right away. He will now work in a TESCO supermarket not far away from the house they now live in. Today (it's Monday) is his first working day, so Michael got up very early. He .... *(möchten)* to be there on time. After breakfast (it was a typical English breakfast with .... *(Maisflocken)*, bacon, baked beans, sausages and .... *(Spiegeleier)* and, of course, ... *(Röstbrot)* and marmalade and plenty of tea with milk and sugar) he took his mountain bike and rode to the local supermarket. A friendly-looking man in a white .... *(Kittel)* stood at the staff entrance of the market. Obviously he was waiting for Michael.

Michael .... *(abschließen)* his bike on a chain and walked over to the man in the white coat. "Good morning, sir. I .... *(annehmen, vermuten)* you are the store manager and you are waiting for me. Is that right?"
The name of the store manager is Mr Willy Wellwood, and he now gave Michael a very friendly welcome: "Good morning, Michael. You are right, I have been waiting for you, but only a few minutes. I am .... *(froh)* to see that you arrived on time. My name is Willy Wellwood, I am the store manager. Please come with me to my office." They walked all the way through the entrance area of the market to the store manager's office where a young lady was already waiting for them. Mr Wellwood now introduced Michael to Sharon Robinson, the assistant manageress of the supermarket. She smiled and stretched out her hand. "How do you do, Michael?" she asked. Michael knew quite well what the only .... *(möglich)* answer to this question during a formal introduction was. Therefore, he took Sharon's hand, shook it and answered: "How do you do, Miss Robinson?" Sharon smiled at him again and asked him to .... *(einfach)* call her Sharon. Now Mr Wellwood turned to Michael again: "All right, Michael, after you have been issued with a proper working dress, Sharon
will show you the market this morning. You will see that it is .... *(ziemlich)* big, all in all we run 25 departments or sections. Sharon will then make a shift roster for you. Remember, in this supermarket we have to work shift .... *(weil)* of our opening hours, but all our staff have every other weekend off, and so will you. Furthermore, Sharon will take the necessary details for your .... *(Personalakte)* which we have to send to London. We also need a .... *(Gesundheitszeugnis)* certificate for you, so we have already arranged for an appointment with a physician. You will see Dr Feelgood (he is .... *(verantwortlich, zuständig)* for health matters) tomorrow morning for a health check. Sharon will tell you when you have to be there and where his .... *(Arztpraxis)* is. And now, Michael, go ahead and look!"
After the introduction, Sharon .... *(bitten)* him to follow her, and so they left the manager's office for a tour round the market. Michael was deeply ....

(beeindruckt). This supermarket was so much bigger than the one he worked for in Germany. Some things were different from German supermarket. There was, for example, a very big sandwich bar in the entrance zone where people could rush in and buy some sandwiches for .... *(Mittagessen)* or tea without having to wait very long at the normal checkouts. This place was crowded. One after the other, they visited all the .... *(verschieden)* departments of the market, and all the time, Sharon gave him much information. She also told him that he should .... *(erkunden)* the market by himself again tomorrow afternoon in order to really familiarize himself with it. Before he knocked off, Sharon told him that he would have to work in the greengrocery department tomorrow morning. This week, he was on the .... *(Frühschicht)*, so he had to be at work fairly early.

Unit 3

Section 1 Texts

Text 1 Practise makes perfect

The situation for the Crockers in their new home was now quite pleasant. His father could walk to work, the barracks were only a few minutes walk away from the house. So there was no need for him to use the car during the week. His mother had been very lucky indeed: She found a job with an import-export company in London right away. Because
5 she can speak English and German fluently, and she has an extra qualification as a business correspondent. Her office is in the City of London, so she takes the commuter train in the mornings and evenings which takes her to London Victoria station. From there, it is only a few minutes ride with the underground (the famous "Tube") to her office. And her job is very well paid. Commuting to work is a very common thing in the U.K., millions of people
10 travel into central London every day to work there.

Michael had spent a few weeks in the greengrocery department and got familiar with the different kinds of vegetables and fruits. But now it was time for a change. This week, he was on the afternoon shift, that meant he could sleep much longer in the morning, something he liked very much. He took it easy, enjoyed his breakfast, went jogging for half an hour,
15 took a shower, got changed and then took his bike to ride to work. He did not know where to work this week, so he went to see Sharon (the assistant store manageress) to find out what he would have to do. Sharon told him that this afternoon he would have to work together with Ginger and Millie, two girls who are responsible for replenishing the shelves in the grocery department. That would give him an ideal opportunity to learn more about
20 the range of products in the market. She also told him where to find the two girls, they would most probably be in the storeroom. He went there and found them immediately. After a short introduction Ginger told him what to do – he had to follow them and push

the trolley with the goods on. The three sales assistants now walked along the shelves and checked the items stacked on the shelves. There were many different items they had to check – tins of baked beans, baked beans with sausages, tins of corned beef, various kinds of soups, Mulligatawny soup, Scotch broth, steak & kidney pie, steak & mushroom pie, custard powder, jars with marmalade and jam etc. Whenever they saw that an item was in low supply they stopped and used their scanner to check the entire stock of this item. Remember, they used an electronic device for it. All they had to do was to make the scanner read the bar code on the edge of the shelf in front of the appropriate item. The scanner then showed the entire number of items in stock on its display. If Ginger found that a particular item was in low supply she simply placed an order by pressing a certain button on the scanner. The rest was then done by the central computer in the admin office. The following morning the items would then be delivered by the big lorry from the central warehouse. When Ginger found that an item on the shelf was in low supply she told Michael to go to the storeroom and fetch sufficient numbers of the missing items. Michael then pushed his trolley to the storeroom and told the storeroom staff what he needed. He then put the items in his trolley and returned to the two girls who were usually waiting for him in front of the shelf. The items were then stacked on the shelf. Michael was kept very busy this afternoon, and before he knew it was time to finish work. When he went home that evening, his feet and his back were aching.

Vocabulary List

pleasant	erfreulich
business correspondent	Fremdsprachenkorrespondent/-in
commute (to, r)	pendeln
commuter	Pendler
city	Innenstadt, auch Großstadt
The City	Stadtteil von London, das Finanzzentrum
enjoy (to, r)	genießen
change	der Wechsel
replenish (to, r)	nachfüllen, auffüllen
opportunity	Gelegenheit
sausage	kleines Würstchen zum Frühstück
Mulligatawny soup	indische Hühnersuppe mit Curry
Scotch broth	Graupensuppe
steak & kidney pie	Pastete mit einem Ragout aus Rindfleisch und Nieren
steak & mushroom pie	Pastete mit einem Ragout aus Rindfleisch und Champignons
custard powder	Soßenpulver für Vanillesoße
device	Vorrichtung, Ding, Gerät
edge	Kante
entire	gesamt
warehouse	Lagerhaus
sufficient	ausreichend

to keep someone busy	jemanden auf Trab halten, beschäftigen
ache (to, r)	wehtun, schmerzen

For the irregular verbs in this story which are all in the past tense please refer to the "ABC of irregular verbs" in the annex of this book.

Text 2 Out of the frying pan, into the fire

Michael woke up with a backache and a muscle ache in his arms. All these boxes and crates he had to move and lift yesterday, and all the stacking! Tinned food is heavy, and people buy lots of it. Especially baked beans sell like hot cakes, people in Britain like them very much, and not only for breakfast but also for tea. Michael was prepared to stack shelves again when he arrived at the market, but when he reported to Sharon this morning she told him that he would have another job to do. Pete had reported sick yesterday, he was on sick leave for the rest of the week. Therefore Michael would have to do Pete's job in the drinks department. Oh dear! Michael remembered well what Pete had told him some days ago – work in the drinks department is not very funny because of the heavy crates that have to be moved there all the time. Now this, his arms and legs and especially his back were still aching from the work he had to do the day before. But Sharon was the boss, so he did not say anything. He put on his white coat and walked over to the drinks department where Bill, the assistant in charge of the department, was already waiting for him. After a brief welcome Bill asked him if he knew how to operate the scanner for stocktaking which Michael answered in the affirmative because he said: "Yes, of course I do, I had to work with it all day yesterday!" "Fine," said Bill, "then here is your job for this afternoon. Check the existing stocks of foreign wines on the shelves and replenish if necessary. We have a separate storeroom for alcoholic drinks, it is behind the storeroom for tinned food. Mary-Rose Smithe is in charge of it, so you will have to report to her if you need something." Michael was relieved. Quite obviously this job was not as hard as the one he had to do yesterday. He expected to have to put single bottles on the shelves, and bottles are not that heavy. So he took the scanner and began to walk along the shelves while he carefully checked the number of wine and sherry bottles on the shelves. He soon found that certain French red wines and also Hock were in low supply, so he took a trolley and went over to the storeroom for drinks where he reported to Mary-Rose Smithe. She already knew what he needed because her computer had received the message from Michael's scanner. When she saw Michael's trolley she began to laugh. "What are you going to do with that tiny little thing?" she asked, pointing at Michael's trolley. "You need something much bigger to pile the crates on!" "What crates?" Michael asked quite surprised, "I thought I have to collect some bottles here!"

35 Mary-Rose smiled and now explained to Michael that wines usually come in crates holding six bottles each, and she gave him a very large platform trolley which was kept in her storeroom for that purpose. There was room for some 54 crates on that trolley! Michael very soon found out that these crates are not much lighter than the crates holding tins of baked beans, for example. Michael now loaded this trolley and pushed it back to his
40 department. Because of its weight, the trolley was difficult to push. All the time, Michael had to make sure that he did not bump into customers or shelves. When he arrived in his department, he was covered with sweat. Now he had to stack the bottles and crates, and he had to go back to the storeroom several times this afternoon. When he went home that evening, the ache in his feet and his back was even worse than the day before.

Vocabulary List

out of the frying pan, into the fire	sinnbildlich: vom Regen in die Traufe
backache	Rückenschmerzen
muscle ache	Muskelkater
to sell like hot cakes	weggehen wie warme Semmeln
tea	hier: warme Mahlzeit am späten Nachmittag
report (to, r)	melden, berichten
to report sick	sich krank melden
to be on sick leave	krankgeschrieben sein
to be in charge of s.th.	für etwas verantwortlich sein
brief	kurz
stocktaking	Bestandsaufnahme, Inventur
foreign	fremd, ausländisch
to be relieved	erleichtert sein
Hock	deutscher Weißwein aus Rheinhessen
tiny	winzig
pile (to, r)	stapeln, übereinanderlegen
pile (the)	der Stapel
purpose	Zweck
platform trolley	Handwagen
bump (to, r)	anrempeln, anstoßen
sweat (the)	Schweiß
enjoy (to, r)	genießen

For the irregular verbs in this story which are all in the past tense please refer to the "ABC of irregular verbs" in the annex of this book.

Comprehension exercise

Please answer the following questions in full sentences.

1. Why was the situation for the Crocker family so pleasant now?
2. Why did Michael's mother get such a good job?
3. What are the advantages of being on the late shift for Michael?
4. How are stocks in Michael's supermarket replenished?
5. How did Michael feel in the evening after his work with Ginger and Millie?
6. When are baked beans mainly eaten?
7. Why didn't Pete come to work?
8. What exactly is "Hock"?
9. What is the difference between a normal shopping trolley and a platform trolley?
10. How would you define a "pile"?

Section 2 Basics

2.1 The range of products in a typical supermarket

Now let us go shopping in the modern TESCO supermarket where Michael works. First of all, we need a trolley, and we have to pay a deposit to get one. You usually have to pay a one-pound coin as a deposit but you will get your money back after you have returned the trolley. The coin must be put in a little drawer at the handle of the trolley. After that you can remove it from the little chain it is attached to. You already know that a supermarket has many departments, so let us visit one department after the other and find out what we can buy there.

- Look at the words in the lists under the names of the departments and translate them.
- Then try to find as many words as possible which also belong to this particular list of items. Write the English word first and then its German meaning. And if you don't know any more words, look them up in the annex of this textbook.

General food – grocery

sugar	____________	salt	____________
flour	____________	olive oil	____________

Vegetables

onion	____________	potato	____________
bean	____________	pea	____________

Fruits

banana	____________	orange	____________
cherry	____________	pear	____________

Bakery

bread	______	toast	______
biscuits	______	muffins	______

Dairy products

milk	______	cheese	______
butter	______	buttermilk	______

At the butcher's/meat

pork	______	beef	______
ham	______	bacon	______

Convenience food

pizza	______		______
	______		______

Fish and seafood

herring	______	tuna fish	______
trout	______	carp	______

Frozen food

fish fingers	______		______
	______		______

Drinks

Coke	______	lemonade	______
water	______	beer	______

Stationery

pencil	______	biro	______
ink	______	crayon	______

Household utensils

broom	______	dustpan	______
mop	______	duster	______

2.2 Means of packaging *Verpackungen*

Many items in a supermarket are packed. This is mainly for hygienic reasons, but also for practical reasons. Packed items are a lot easier to handle, just think of loose foods such as sugar or flour. The list below shows some of the most common means of packaging.

packaging	typically used for	
wooden crate	vegetables, fruits	
small crate	vegetables, fruits	
mesh bag	oranges, tomatoes, potatoes	
plastic tray	strawberries, raspberries	
egg carton	eggs	
pouch	rice	
bag	sugar, flour, rice, sweets	
package	spaghetti	
cup	yoghurt, cream	
tin	vegetables, fruit	
carton	milk, fruit juice	
tube	mustard, mayonaise, toothpaste	
cheese box	soft cheese	
flat tray	meat	
jar	jam, marmalade, honey	
bottle (glass, plastic)	liquids, drinks	
spray can	cream, household products	
tub	margarine	
pack	cigarettes	
bar	chocolate, soap	
box	chocolates	
drink box	soft drinks	
crate	bottles	
plastic film	vegetables, fruits	

Vocabulary List

wooden crate	=	Holzkiste
small crate	=	Spankiste
mesh bag	=	Netz
tray	=	Schale
pouch	=	Beutel

2.3 Advertising

Flyers, leaflets & advertisements

Two weeks later, Michael sat in Sheila Robertson's office. His problems with his back and his aching muscles were long forgotten. He now had a job in the admin office where he mainly worked at the computer. Mrs Robertson has a half-time job, she only works in the mornings and she is responsible for the advertising of the market. Advertising is very important in the retail business. Shops usually require direct contact with their customers in order to inform them of the products they have for sale, and this is usually done by means of flyers and leaflets which are directly put in letter boxes, but also by putting advertisements in the local newspapers. Most of the advertising material comes from the company headquarters in London, but sometimes they also issue their own leaflets and flyers which are then distributed to all households in the town. This is especially the case when the market has to react quickly to special offer campaigns of the competing supermarkets in town of which there are two or three. In such cases Mr Wellwood selects some similar items from their range of products which are then offered at unbeatable prices. Mr Wellwood usually just makes a list of the items he intends to put on special offer, and Sheila has a special computer program which she uses to design the flyer. These pages of the flyer are then sent by e-mail to the local printer who prints them overnight and has them distributed. The following morning, these flyers are in the letter boxes of all houses and flats in town. Mr Morrison also pays very close attention to the flyers the other supermarkets distribute, and so she always knows what is going on. This afternoon, however, Michael was on his own in the office, and when the daily mail was brought in he sorted it and found the following flyers of their competitors in the mail. Have a look at them:

Spring Clean
Best Buys
Offers Valid 9th March to 22nd March 2009
new
FAIRY
PLATINUM
Trial Price
£3.32
22 pack
Save £3.32
100s of Offers
HALF PRICE
PRICE CRUNCH
HALF PRICE
£1.55
77p
500ml
Save 78p
Flash
HALF PRICE
£1.94
97p
1 litre
Save 97p
Flash
HALF PRICE
£8
£4
each
Save £4
HALF PRICE
buy 3 ready meals for only
£5
for details. Subject to availability. Selected stores only.
Save up to £61 with these great deals
BIGGER PACK BETTER VALUE
Tropicana
pure premium
Original
HELLMANN'S
REAL MAYONNAISE
Cadbury creme egg
FLORA
SENSATIONS
CODORNIU
Save £1.75
1/2 price
Only £1.74 each
Save 98p
2 for £2
£1.49 each
Save £6
1/2 price
Only £5.99
Earn nectar points too

Vocabulary List

leaflet	Prospekt
flyer	Flugblatt
advertising	Werbung
advertisement	die Anzeige, Annonce
half-time job	Halbzeitbeschäftigung
distribute (to, r)	verteilen
competing	konkurrierend
competitor	Konkurrent
special offer	Sonderangebot
s.th. is on special offer	etwas ist im Sonderangebot
design (to, r)	hier: entwerfen

Section 3 Brush up your grammar

3.1 How to ask questions *Fragen stellen*

In der deutschen Sprache haben wir es bei der Fragestellung einfach. Wir stellen einfach im Satz die Positionen von persönlichem Fürwort und Verb um (das nennt sich Umkehrung) und fügen ein Fragezeichen an. In der englischen Sprache müssen wir dagegen das Hilfsverb "to do" verwenden, um eine Frage bilden zu können.

Beispiel:

Statement/Aussage: William drives a new car.
Subjekt Prädikat Objekt

Wenn wir hier nach der Satzergänzung "new car" fragen wollen, dann muss diese Frage wie folgt formuliert werden:

Question/Frage: Does William drive a new car?
Subjekt Prädikat Objekt

Hier sehen wir, dass das Hilfsverb "to do" entsprechend der Form "he" (dritte Person, Einzahl, männlich) als "does" verwendet wird. Das Vollverb im Satz wird aber jetzt nicht mehr konjugiert (das haben wir ja bereits mit dem Hilfsverb getan), sondern es wird in seiner Grundform "drive" verwendet.

Wir sehen außerdem, dass die Reihenfolge Subjekt – Prädikat – Objekt bei der Fragestellung erhalten geblieben ist. Das ist eine Eigenheit der englischen Sprache, die es in der deutschen Sprache so nicht gibt.

Daher muss immer an die Regel S P O gedacht werden.

Ausnahme:

Die Ausnahme von der obigen Regel ist die Verwendung des Hilfsverbs "to be". Hier können wir die Frage genauso wie im Deutschen durch Umkehrung bilden.

Beispiel:

Statement/Aussage:	William is a shop assistant.
	Subjekt Prädikat Objekt

Wenn wir hier nach der Satzergänzung "shop assistant" fragen wollen, dann kann diese Frage einfach wie folgt formuliert werden:

Question/Frage: Is William a shop assistant?

3.2 Negation *Verneinung*

Auch für die Verneinung brauchen wir das Hilfsverb "to do".

Beispiel:

Statement/Aussage:	The shop assistant works on Monday.
Negation/Verneinung:	The shop assistant does not work on Sunday.

Ausnahme:

Die Ausnahme von der obigen Regel ist auch hier die Verwendung des Hilfsverbs "to be". Hier können wir die Verneinung genauso wie im Deutschen mithilfe des Wortes "not" bilden.

Beispiel:

Statement/Aussage:	My uncle is a butcher.
Negation/Verneinung:	My uncle is not a butcher.

Excersise

Form questions like in the above examples. Use the simple present tense only.

1 Michael's mother works as a business correspondent.
2 Cauliflower is on special offer today.
3 Michael drives a used car.
4 I know Michael and his family.
5 Michael's father is an army officer.
6 Bananas come from South America and Africa.
7 Michael's sisters like Black Forest gateau.
8 Mr Wellwood reads the mail in the morning.
9 Michael likes to work as a cashier.
10 Michael's grandmother is a very good cook.

3.3 Question tags *Der umkehrende Anhang an eine Frage*

Eine Eigenheit der englischen Sprache ist die Verwendung von sogenannten "tags". Ein "tag" ist ein Anhang an den Satz. Insbesondere wenn wir eine einfache Frage mit "ja" oder "nein" beantworten, sollten wir ein "tag" hinzufügen, um höflich zu sein.

Beispiele:

Frage	Positive Antwort	Negative Antwort
Do you like music?	Yes, I do.	No, I don't (do not).
Are you hungry?	Yes, I am.	No, I'm not (am not).

Die Briten verwenden besonders "tags", welche die Botschaft umkehren.

Beispiele:

Today is a lovely day, isn't it?
The sun isn't too hot, is it?
You can sit outside today, can't you?
You don't like hamburgers, do you?
Sharon lives in Nottingham, doesn't she?
We must not be late, must we?

Wichtige Regel:

Nach einem bejahten Satz benutzen wir ein verneinendes "tag", und nach einem verneinten Satz benutzen wir ein bejahendes "tag". Wir bilden das "tag" immer mithilfe des Hilfsverbs im Satz. Falls es kein Hilfsverb im Satz gibt, bilden wir das "tag" mit "to do".

Exercise

Fill in the missing question tag.

1 This is an easy and useful exercise, ______________________ ?

2 You can't make many mistakes, ______________________ ?

3 The Swansea City AFC is a very good football club, ______________________ ?

4 A football team consists of eleven players, ______________________ ?

5 Michael's parents are not at home, ______________________ ?

6 His father usually eats a full English breakfast, ______________________ ?

7 He is always very tired in the morning, ______________________ ?

8 Michael does not know the results of the last cricket match, ______________________ ?

9 He keeps all his certificates in a file, ______________________ ?

10 Cows give milk, ______________________ ?

11 TESCO is not a small supermarket, ______________________ ?

12 Fish can not fly, ______________________ ?

13 Michael does not have a backache, ______________________ ?

14 Edinburgh is not the capital of the UK, ______________________ ?

15 The British love their five o'clock tea, ______________________ ?

16 British people are very polite, ______________________ ?

17 Cheese is made from milk, ______________________ ?

18 We must not disturb the lessons, ______________________ ?

19 Dad can not repair our radio, ______________________ ?

20 School does not always finish at 1 pm, ______________________ ?

21 The Crockers are on holiday, ______________________ ?

22 You know enough about advertising, ______________________ ?

23 These apples do not come from France, ______________________ ?

24 We can not understand Chinese, ______________________ ?

25 This exercise is boring now, ______________________ ?

Section 4 Practise your word power

4.1 Exercise Word groups

Put each of the words below into the correct list. Use each word only once! Can you think of more words to add to each list?

milk apple peach melon coconut peppers celery banana sugar feta cheese paprika chocolate apple beer pear raspberries wine peppers coffee radish lemonade apricot cucumber potatoes cream Coke Swiss cheese salt oil peppers sugar strawberries pear vinegar parsley flour

1 Brown

....
....
....
....
....
....

2 Red

....
....
....
....
....
....

3 Green

....
....
....
....
....
....

4 White

....
....
....
....
....
....

5 Yellow

....
....
....
....
....
....

6 Liquid

....
....
....
....
....
....

4.2 Exercise Odd man out

Only one answer is right. Which one is ot?

1 One of these is not round. Which one is it?
a ball b wheel c cucumber
d disc e apple

2 Veal is meat from a
a sheep b pig c horse
d calf e rabbit

3 One of these is not sweet. Which one is it?
a chocolate b liquorice c honey
d candy e goose

4 Honey is collected by
a ants b bees c ladybirds
d caterpillars e butterflies

5 One of these is not part of a computer system. Which one is it?
a mouse b monitor c crisps
d printer e scanner

6 One of these is not a vegetable. Which one is it?
a cabbage b cauliflower c peas
d spinach e pears

7 One of these is a drink but also a meal. Which one is it?
a tea b lunch c snack
d dinner e supper

8 The colour of a mushroom is
a blue b white c black
d violet e green

9 One of these has nothing to do with whisky. Which one is it?
a liquid b Scotland c distillery
d barley e sweet

10 The favourite snack of the British is
a raw fish and rice b fish & chips c fish & crisps
d herring in cream sauce e fish and jacket potatoes

11 One of these does not grow in the ground. Which one is it?
a peanut b carrot c potato
d asparagus e walnut

12 The part of your salary that goes to the government is the
a wages b salary c income tax
d bonus e profit

13 Which of these can be bitter?
a cucumber b avocado c potato
d almond e cauliflower

14 The container jam and marmalade are sold in is a
a bottle b bag c jar
d net e sack

15 A big bird the British eat on Christmas Day is the
a hen b chicken c goose
d duck e turkey

16 Where would you have to go if you wanted to buy Black Forest gateau?
a cheese counter b florist c baker
d butcher e grocer

17 One of these does not grow in Europe. Which one is it?
a tomato b potato c cabbage
d banana e radish

18 The informal way of saying "I finish my work now" is
a I knock off b I fall asleep c I go on
d I am fed up e I go elsewhere

19 One of these is different from the others - it does not burn. Which one is it?
a wood b coal c fuel oil
d paper e stone

20 The head of state of the United Kingdom is
a Gordon Brown b Tony Blair c H.M. The Queen
d Prince Charles e Barack Obama

4.3 Exercise Definitions

half Easter Sunday minced meat towel potato checkout at once pumpkin grass summer cucumber tube bottle afternoon round Tuesday Reunification Day uncle tap pharmacy

1 a long green vegetable (slightly bent) which we use for making salad
2 what the cow likes to eat
3 the hottest of the four seasons of the year
4 the second working day after Sunday
5 the period of time after 12.00 a. m
6 30 minutes are a....... an hour
7 a brown vegetable that grows in the ground
8 The second day after Good Friday is
9 A container made of glass for liquid food
10 Finely chopped pork or beef is called
11 the place where customers pay for their shopping
12 After you have washed your hands, you dry them with a
13 The biggest vegetable we know is the
14 The device in a bathroom that gives water is the
15 the shape of peas and cherries
16 Toothpaste usually comes in a
17 Your father's brother is your
18 Another word for "immediately" is
19 A shop where you can buy medicine is a
20 The 3rd of October is

4.4 Exercise Fill the gaps

Practise makes perfect

The situation for the Crockers in their new home was now quite .... *(erfreulich)*. His father could .... *(zu Fuss gehen)* to work, the barracks were only a few minutes walk away from the house. So there was no need for him to use the car during the week. His mother had been very lucky indeed, she found a job with an import-export company in London right away .... *(weil)* she can speak English and German fluently, and she has an extra qualification as a business correspondent. Her office is in the City of London, so she takes the commuter train in the mornings and evenings which takes her to London Victoria station. From there, it is .... *(nur)* a few minutes travel with the underground (the famous "Tube") to her office. And her job is very well paid. .... *(Pendeln)* to work is a very common thing in the U.K., millions of people travel into central London every day to work there.

Michael had spent a few weeks in the .... *(Obst- und Gemüseabteilung)* department and got very familiar with the different kinds of vegetables and fruits. But now it was time for a change. This week, he was on the .... *(Nachmittagsschicht)* shift, that meant he could sleep much longer in the morning, something he liked very much. He took it easy, ... *(genießen)* his breakfast, went jogging for half an hour, took a .... *(Dusche)*, got changed and then took his bike to ride to work. He did not know where to work this week, so he went to see Sharon (the assistant store manageress) to find out what he would have to do. Sharon told him that this afternoon he would have to work together with Ginger and Millie, two girls who are .... *(verantwortlich)* for replenishing the shelves in the grocery department. That would give him an ideal opportunity to learn more about the .... *(Produktpalette)* in the market. She .... (auch) told him where to find the two girls, they would most probably be in the storeroom. He went there and found them .... *(unmittelbar, sofort)*. After a short introduction Ginger told him what to do – he had to follow them and .... *(schieben)* the trolley with the goods on. The three sales assistants now walked along the shelves and checked the items stacked on the shelves. There were many .... *(verschiedene)* items they had to check – tins of baked beans, baked beans with .... *(Würstchen)*, tins of corned beef, various kinds of soups Mulligatawny soup, Scotch broth, steak & kidney pie, steak & mushroom pie, custard powder, ... *(Schraubgläser)* with marmalade and .... *(Konfitüre)* etc. Whenever they saw that an item was in low supply they stopped and used their scanner to check the entire stock of this item. Remember, they used an electronic .... *(Vorrichtung, Gerät)* for it. All they had to do was to make the scanner read the .... *(Strichcode)* on the edge of the shelf in front of the appropriate item. The scanner then showed the entire number of items in stock on its display. If Ginger found that a particular item was in low supply she simply placed an .... *(Bestellung)* by pressing a certain button on the scanner. The rest was then done by the central computer in the admin office. The following morning the items would then be delivered by the big .... *(Lkw)* from the central warehouse. When Ginger found that an item on the shelf was in low supply she told Michael to go to the storeroom and .... *(holen)* sufficient numbers of the missing items. Michael then pushed his trolley to the storeroom and told the storeroom staff what he needed. He then put the items in his trolley and .... *(zurückkehren)* to the two girls who were usually waiting for him in front of the shelf. The items were then stacked on the shelf. Michael was kept very busy this afternoon, and before he .... *(wissen)* it was time to finish work. When he went home that evening, his feet and his back were aching.

Unit 4

Section 1 Texts

Text 1 Money makes the world go round

Michael knew quite well that one day he would have to work at one of the checkouts of the supermarket because it was part of his internal training programme. But up to now, he had always tried to avoid it because he
5 was not yet really familiar with British money. On a few occasions he had to work at one of the checkouts under supervision, but never on his own. But this morning Susan, the checkout supervisor, called Michael into her little office near the checkout area and told him that one
10 of the cashiers (her name is Marianne) from the morning shift reported sick this morning and she would be on sick leave all week long. Susan asked Michael if he could stand in for Marianne this week because she was very short of cashiers. Most of the cashiers work shift because during
15 the day not all checkouts have to be manned. It is mainly the late afternoon and the early evening when it gets really busy at the checkouts. As Marianne works morning shifts only, Michael would only have to work at the checkout until noon. Michael, however, was a little bit worried and told Susan about the problems he had with British money.
20 "Come on, Michael, don't be a coward, I know you can do it" encouraged him Susan. And then she added: "I need your help! And the money is not the problem, all checkouts are equipped with the most modern scanners and most customers pay by credit card or

banker's card anyway. Very few people pay cash these days!" "All right, Susan" said Michael, "you have talked me into it. What exactly do I have to do?" Now Susan took him to a
25 currently inactive checkout and showed him everything. "It is easy, really", she told him again. "The most important thing is to make sure that all items are properly scanned, one after the other. You will hear a clearing signal the moment the item has been scanned, then you can scan the next one. Sometimes the system cannot identify the bar code properly, but then the system will warn you. And if it can't read the bar code at all, you will tap the
30 item number which is below the bar code in yourself, but it does not happen very often. Relax!" She then showed Michael how to operate the card reader at the electronic payment terminal for credit cards, banker's cards and other plastic money and also how to accept cheques. She also gave him a list with all the credit cards the company accepted. Then she explained the operation of the scanner to him. "Don't worry, Michael, I will stay with you
35 all day and I will help you whenever you need it," she said. This gave Michael some more self-confidence. At the beginning, he worked a little bit slowly, but all went well, and in the early afternoon at the end of his shift Michael balanced without any problems. He was very proud.

Vocabulary List

avoid (to, r)	vermeiden
to be familiar with s.th.	mit etwas vertraut sein
occasion	Gelegenheit
to talk s.o. into s.th.	jmd. überreden
to be on sick leave	krankgeschrieben sein
man (to, r)	besetzen (Arbeitsplatz)
worry (to, r)	sich sorgen
coward	Feigling
pay cash	bar bezahlen
relax (to, r)	entspannen
accept (to, r)	annehmen
self-confidence	Selbstvertrauen
balance (to, r)	Kasse abstimmen
proud	stolz

For the irregular verbs in this story which are mostly in the past tense please refer to the "ABC of irregular verbs" in the annex of this book.

Text 2 Let me help you, please!

This was Michael's third day at the checkout, and he slowly began to get used to the job, he even began to like it. So early in the morning before the market opened, Michael reported to the checkout supervisor (today a young man named Adrian was doing the job because Susan had a day off) to collect the box with the change. He checked it and then took it to the checkout where he put it into the drawer of the cash register. Then he tapped in his identification number to start the program. He also had to enter the amount of cash he had in the money drawer so that the system could always work out how much money he had in his cash register. He also needed that figure to balance in the evening or whenever he had to hand the checkout over to another cashier. Michael made himself comfortable in his chair and waited for the first customer to come. This was a lady with a trolley full of shopping which gave Michael a good opportunity to practise his skills as a cashier. The lady paid by credit card, so he didn't have to handle any cash, it was a simple procedure. All he had to do was to pull the card through the card reader and wait for the system to clear the amount. He returned the card to the customer and thanked her for doing her shopping in this particular market. The morning was fairly quiet which gave Michael enough time to improve his skills. At 11 o'clock he was relieved by another colleague. He now had an hour off. It was time for a good lunch, he rushed to the sandwich bar where he bought a cheese and onion sandwich and another one filled with crispy bacon and tomatoes. After he had taken over the checkout again after his lunch break, he suddenly saw something very unusual. A group of boys and girls in uniform turned up and they positioned themselves at the ends of all checkouts. What could this be? Fortunately Adrian, the checkout supervisor, stood next to his checkout, so he asked him. "Oh yes, Michael, I forgot to tell you. It is Wednesday afternoon, and on Wednesdays the Scouts come here to work as packers for the customers. These here are Wolf Cubs and Brownies, young boys and girls who wish to become Boy Scouts and Girl Guides. They help our customers to pack all their shopping into carrier bags, and they always get a few pence for their help which they collect for their annual summer camp. The customers like them, so we let them do it." After a short time, the Scouts eagerly began to help the customers at the checkouts, they skilfully took all the stuff from the conveyor band and put it in carrier bags, and they even helped customers with full trolleys to push them to the car park. Michael then did not have much more time to watch the Scouts, it slowly got very busy. Most people had finished work, and now they went shopping. At five o'clock, he was relieved by another cashier. He took the money box out of the drawer, checked out at the terminal and took the box over to the supervisor's office. The supervisor already had Michael's balance available (he has a special computer program for it), so they counted the money in Michael's cashbox – and once again, he balanced straight away.

Vocabulary List

report (to, r)	melden
drawer	Schublade
cash register	Registrierkasse
enter (to, r)	hier: eingeben
comfortable (adj.)	bequem
opportunity	Gelegenheit
return (to, r)	hier: zurückgeben
relieve (to, r)	ablösen
procedure	Verfahren
crispy	knusprig
Scout	Pfadfinder
Wolf Cub	Wölfling (Jungpfadfinder)
Brownie	Jungpfadfinderin
pence	Mehrzahl von "penny"
eager (adj.)	eifrig
conveyor band	Laufband an der Kasse
balance (the)	Kassenbestand, Saldo, Kontostand

For the irregular verbs in this story which are mostly in the past tense please refer to the "ABC of irregular verbs" in the annex of this book.

Comprehension exercise

Please answer the following questions in full sentences.

1 Why did Michael try to avoid work at a checkout?
2 What is the work system for cashiers and why is it so?
3 How do customers pay?
4 What is a checkout equipped with?
5 What does a cashier have to do in the evening after he/she finished work?
6 How often had Michael worked at a checkout so far?
7 Who is responsible for the cashiers and their work?
8 Describe how customers usually carry their shopping.
9 What happens on Wednesdays in Michael's supermarket?
10 How do the Scouts help the customers in the market and why?

Section 2 Basics

2.1 The money in the United Kingdom

Until 1971, the British money was a very complicated and difficult affair, foreigners often could not understand it. The money in the United Kingdom was and is called the "pound sterling". This is a very old word, more than 1.200 years old, and it originally meant that it was a bar or ingot of sterling silver which weighed one pound. Because a bar was heavy and difficult to handle, the silver was used to make coins. And because it was a lot of silver the result logically was also a lot of coins it was 240 silver "pennies" or "pence". Later there was also a larger coin which was called the "shilling". One pound had 20 shillings, and one shilling had 12 pence, which all together came to 240 pence to the pound. This system was used until 1971 (15th of February 1971 – Decimalisation Day). Then the pound was made a decimal currency, that means that one pound simply has 100 pence. The problem with British coins was that they usually did not have figures or numbers on them, just words. So if you did not understand the word on the coin, you did not know how much it was worth. But that has changed. Today, some of the coins in Britain bear figures which tell how much they are worth. But not all of them do. The banknotes were and still are easier to understand. There are currently pound sterling or English pound banknotes to the value of £5, £10, £20 and £50. Until approx. 1985, banknotes to the value of £1 were also in circulation. But then they were replaced by £1 coins. The banknotes in Scotland and Northern Ireland are different from the English pound banknotes in England and Wales, but the coins are the same in the whole of the U.K. Currently there are coins to the value of one penny (1d), two pence (2d), five pence (5d), 10 pence (10d), 20 pence (20d), 50 pence (50d), one pound (£1) and two pounds (£2).

Note

When people talk about an even amount of money (e. g. £5), they say "five pounds". So they add an "s" to the word "pound" in the plural. But if they talk about any amount of pounds followed by an amount of pence (e. g. £5.50), they would say "five pound fifty", so here they do not add the "s".

Vocabulary List

foreigner	Fremder, Ausländer
bar, ingot	Barren aus Edelmetall
coin	Münze
currency	Währung
amount	hier: Geldbetrag

Note

Achtung: In der deutschen Sprache sagen wir: Das kostet 50 Euro, 20 amerikanische Dollar, 10 englische Pfund etc. Wir hängen also kein Mehrzahl-"s" an die Währungsbezeichnung. Im Englischen dagegen sagen wir: It costs 50 Euros, 20 American dollars, 10 English pounds etc., sofern es sich um Beträge ohne Dezimalstellen hinter dem Komma handelt.

2.2 Credit cards – plastic money conquers the world

Payment without cash is not a new thing. The first credit card was "invented" in the United States in the year 1950. The businessman Frank McNamara created it after he had forgotten his wallet with his money when he went for dinner in a nice restaurant. He then founded the "Diners Club". Originally the use of the first credit card was restricted to 27 restaurants, as its name implies, it was to be used for eating out or dining. In the first year, the club had only 200 members, but it quickly grew. In 1958, American Express followed with their own card, and in 1958 came the first Visa credit card, and the Master Card followed in 1966.
Today the number of different credit cards and charge cards (which are almost similar to credit cards) cannot be counted any more, and there are other customer cards with similar functions, too. Credit cards are usually issued by banks or credit unions, their shape and size is now standardized.

Vocabulary List

invent (to, r)	erfinden
create (to, r)	schaffen
found (to, r)	gründen
dinner	Abendessen
imply (to, r)	andeuten
grow (to, ir)	wachsen
similar	ähnlich, gleichartig
shape	Form
standardize (to, r)	normen
standardized	genormt

2.3 Money and the bank

Nº 049198
19
£
S Nº 049198
35418
19
Lloyds Bank Limited
Spilsby.
Pay
or Order
£
London Office, 71, Lombard Street, E.C.3.

The British banking system differs from the German system: There are no equivalents to our "Sparkasse" and "Volksbank". There are four big banks which more or less dominate the banking scene. These are Lloyds TSB, the National Westminster Bank (NatWest), Barclays Bank and the Royal Bank of Scotland. These banks operate a large number of branches in the entire U.K. with thousands of ATMs. It is as normal for a Briton to have a bank account as it is for a German. The main type of account is the current account, but many customers also use a savings account or a deposit account to save money, and of course you can also borrow money from a bank which is called a bankloan or loan. Most payments in the U.K. are still made by cheque. Cheques are much more important than here in Germany. The credit card, of course, becomes more and more popular. Building societies also play an important role in the banking business. They usually offer the same kind of service as the "normal" banks, but they usually offer lower service charges and longer opening hours.

Vocabulary List

equivalent	Gegenstück, hier: entsprechendes Institut
dominate (to, r)	beherrschen
entire	ganz, vollständig, gesamt
ATM	Geldautomat
Briton	Brite, Einwohner von Großbritannien
current account	Girokonto
savings account	Sparkonto
loan	Kredit
payment	Zahlung
building society	Bausparkasse
service charges	Kontoführungsgebühr

2.4. Measures and weights

Another strange thing is the story of weights and measures that are used in the United Kingdom. The British used so-called imperial measures and weights which differed very much from the metric measures and weights which we are used to. Since 1967 the British government has been trying to adopt the metric system, but the British simply do not want it, and that is why both systems are now in use in the country. It would go too far to describe all the imperial weights and measures that are used but here are some of the most important ones:

English designation	metric equivalent	German meaning
ounce	~ 28 g	Unze
pound	454 g	Pfund
gallon	~ 4,5 l	Gallone
pint	~ 0,56 l	Pinte
yard	~ 0,9 m	Yard
mile	~ 1.600 m	Landmeile

Officially, these old or so-called "imperial" measures should have been replaced by metric measures, but this is often not the case. People simply don't want the new "European" measures, they want to retain the old system.

In the meantime, a compromise is often used. The old designation (e. g. 8 oz) is retained, and the new declaration of weight in grams is also on the label.

Vocabulary List

measure	Mass
weight	Gewicht
strange	merkwürdig
imperial measures	brit. Maße (die "Maße des Weltreiches")
differ (to, r)	unterscheiden
adopt (to, r)	annehmen, einführen
replace (to, r)	ersetzen
retain (to, r)	beibehalten
label	Etikett

Section 3 Brush up your grammar

3.1 MANY or MUCH – A FEW or A LITTLE?

Die Wörter "much/many" und "a few/a little" sagen uns etwas über die Menge aus und ob es sich um große oder kleine Mengen handelt. Wir benutzen "many" und "a few" für Dinge, die man zählen kann und "much" und "a little" für Dinge, die man nicht zählen kann.

Beispiele: There is much butter in the fridge but not many eggs.
Please go and buy a little butter and a few eggs.

große Menge	kleine Menge	Erkennungsmerkmal	Beispiele
many	a few	Die Dinge sind zählbar. > You can count them.	books, people, tins, apples, …
much	a little	Die Dinge sind nicht zählbar. > You can not count them.	water, tea, beer, food, rain, sand, …

Normalerweise können wir Einheiten, die wir nicht zählen können (wie Flüssigkeiten, Zeit, Geld, Spass, Ärger oder auch z. B. Sand) zählbar machen, wenn wir eine Maßeinheit dafür finden, z. B. zwei Liter Wasser, drei Stunden, fünf Säcke Sand, ein Korb an Lebensmitteln, drei Tassen Tee, drei Gläser Bier oder einige Regentropfen. In diesen Fällen können wir das Maß oder die Maßeinheit zählen, nicht die Sache selbst.

Exercise:

Try to find out whether the things are countable or not. Fill in "much" or "many".

1 I have .... money in my bank account, and I have .... coins in my purse.

2 This farmer owns .... ground, and he has .... cows and .... sheep.

3 It will take .... hours to repair that car, but I don't have .... time.

4 My father likes to drink .... tea with .... pieces of sugar in it.

5 Father likes tea very .... but he does not take .... milk in it.

6 Yesterday we went to a party where we met .... people and had .... fun.

7 Don't drink too .... it is no good for you.

8 Drinking too .... will always cause you .... problems.

9a My friend likes to go to .... parties where he takes .... drinks.

9b My friend likes to go to .... parties where he drinks .... beer.

10 He usually drinks .... beer and .... Cokes.

11 Sometimes my friend doesn't drink .... beers.

12 I can eat very .... and sometimes I eat .... sandwiches.

13 I never eat .... meat, but I usually eat .... rolls with .... jam on them.

14 The weather forecast said that there will be .... rain tomorrow.

15 I think the forecast is right because I can see .... clouds in the sky.

16 My old car has .... defects, and it consumes .... petrol.

17 This year in July, we had .... sun, so there were .... insects.

18 Don't talk that ....! Too .... of the things you say are rubbish!

19 There were .... clouds in the sky and there was .... snow on the ground.

20. There were .... discussions about the problems in the country, and they were always loaded with .... emotion.

3.2 Some or any?

"Some" drückt aus, dass etwas unbestimmt, aber tatsächlich vorhanden ist. Es steht im bejahten Satz.

Beispiele: Help yourself to some biscuits.
Would you like some tea?

"Any" drückt im Gegensatz zu "some" aus, dass etwas nicht oder nicht sicher vorhanden ist. Es steht daher immer im verneinten Satz und in Fragen, und es steht sehr oft in Fällen, in denen wir im Deutschen das Zusatzwort "überhaupt" verwenden.

Beispiele: Is there any tea left in the pot?
No, we have never had any of these in stock.

3.3 Make, take or do?

Die Verben "to do" und "to make" haben nicht dieselbe Bedeutung. Wir benutzen "to make", wenn etwas neu hergestellt wird, was vorher nicht da war im Sinne von "produzieren".

Beispiele: I make a cup of tea.
I never make a mistake.

Wir benutzen das Verb "to do", wenn wir etwas bearbeiten oder verbessern, was schon vorhanden ist.

Beispiele: I do my hair.
She does her work.

Wichtig: Wir müssen immer "to do" verwenden, wenn wir von Arbeit oder Geschäft reden.

Beispiele: I do my job.
I like to do business with this customer.
He does his homework.

Ein schwieriges Wort ist "to take". Wir benutzen es häufig in Fällen, in denen wir in der deutschen Sprache "machen" verwenden.

Beispiele:	ein Foto machen	to **take** a photo
	einen Spaziergang machen	to **take** a walk
	eine Fahrt machen	to **take** a trip
	eine Prüfung machen	to **take** a test
	Notizen machen	to **take** notes
	eine Pause machen	to **take** a break
	duschen	to **take** a shower
	ein Risiko eingehen	to **take** a risk
	Mut fassen	to **take** courage
	Zeit erfordern	to **take** time

Exercise:

Fill in "make", "take" or "do".

1 After I get up in the morning I usually .... breakfast. *(Eier braten, Tee kochen etc.)*

2 Please .... me a favour and .... me a cup of tea. .... it quickly.

3 After school, pupils and students usually have to .... their homework.

4 The circus clown stood in front of the audience and .... a bow.

5 The teacher reached for his red note book and .... a note of the naughty pupil.

6 Father always .... his camera with him, he likes to .... photos of funny scenes.

7 Tomorrow I have to .... my driving test, it .... me nervous.

8 After you have .... some hard work, you may .... a break.

9 After a hard day in the office, I like to .... a walk in the evening.

10 In this company, we like to .... business with friendly customers.

11 When she gets up in the morning, she usually .... her hair first.

12 .... not hesitate .... the decision right now.

14 Volkswagen cars are usually .... in Germany.

15 It .... not .... much difference whether you .... it today or tomorrow.

16 It will .... a lot of time to repair this machine.

17 I never .... any mistakes, I .... my job properly!

18 When I come home from work, I usually .... a shower first before I .... other things.

19 Last week, we .... a trip to Hanover where we .... new friends.

20 He tried to .... all the preparations, but he could not .... everything himself.

21 Parachuting is very dangerous, do not .... such a risk!

22 She .... all her courage and jumped out of the aircraft.

23 No, I do not .... any sports, I prefer to .... it easy.

3.4 The CONTINUOUS FORM *Die Verlaufsform*

In der englischen Sprache gibt es zwei grundlegende Formen in allen Zeiten: Die "Simple Form" und die "continuous form" (Verlaufsform). Diese Sonderform der Bildung eines Verbs gibt es in der deutschen Sprache nicht, wir können den Verlauf einer Handlung nur durch eine Umschreibung (z. B.: jetzt gerade, jetzt im Moment) erläutern. In der englischen Sprache dagegen können wird durch eine Abänderung des Verbs genau anzeigen, dass eine Handlung in diesem Moment stattfindet. Das nennen wir Verlaufsform: "the continuous form".

Die Grundregel lautet wie folgt:

(to) be (entsprechend konjugiert) + Verb (Grundform) + Endung ing

Beispiel: At the moment I am reading a book. Usually I read magazines.
Dinah was wearing a dress last night. Usually she wore jeans.

Die Tabelle zeigt, wie wir diese "continuous form" bilden:

Bildung

Aussage	Beispiel	Bildung
present tense	Michael's parents are working. He is looking at the label.	to be + verb (Grundform) + ing
past tense	Mr Wellwood was reading a fax. Customers were waiting at the checkout.	

Da die continuous form mit "to be" gebildet wird, bilden wir Fragen durch Inversion (Umstellung).

Frage	Beispiel	Bildung
present tense	Are Michael's parents working? Is he looking at the label?	to be + subject + verb+ing
past tense	Was Mr Wellwood reading a fax? Were the customers waiting at the checkout?	

Um negative Aussagen zu machen, stellen wir ein "not" zwischen die Form von "to be" und die Verbform.

Verneinung	Beispiel	Bildung
present tense	Michael's parents are not working. He is not looking at the label.	to be + not + verb+ing
past tense	Mr Wellwood was not reading a fax. Customers were not waiting at the checkout.	

Schreibweise:

Das –e am Ende eines Verbs entfällt, wenn die Endsilbe –ing angehängt wird:
example: to come – coming, to strike – striking, to drive – driving, to invite - inviting

Verben, die auf einer kurzen betonten Silbe mit einem Konsonanten enden oder nur aus einer kurzen Silbe bestehen, verdoppeln den Konsonanten.

example: to begin – beginning, to forget – forgetting, to hit – hitting, to stop – stopping

EXERCISE

Please put the verbs in brackets into the present continuous form.
Form questions and negations.

1 Michael (to sleep) in his room. (kitchen)
2 Many people (to do) their shopping. (work)
3 I (to train) English grammar. (vocabulary)

Now put the verbs in brackets into the past continuous form and again form questions and negative sentences.

4 Many young people (to do) a practical in their last holidays. (at the weekend)
5 Mr Wellwood (to serve) a customer at 9 o'clock. (8 o'clock)
6 I (to meet) some friends in a pub. (at school)

Section 4 Practise your word power

4.1 Exercise Word groups

Put each of the words below into the correct list. Use each word only once!
Can you think of more words to add to each list?

wine wine wine jam jam nuts vinegar vinegar mustard mustard honey honey honey toffee toffee toffee chili sugar milk bones lemon chocolate butter water oil pepper cheese cheese oil pickles paprika gherkins curry lime juice horseradish juice

1 Liquid

....
....
....
....
....
....

2 Solid/hard

....
....
....
....
....
....

3 Sweet

....
....
....
....
....
....

4 Sour

....
....
....
....
....
....

5 Hot (spicy)

....
....
....
....
....
....

6 Soft

....
....
....
....
....
....

4.2 Exercise Odd man out

Only one answer is right. Which one is it?

1 One of these does not come from a dairy. Which one is it?
a cream b milk c butter
d silk e curd

2 Venison is meat from
a sheep b deer c horse
d calf e rabbit

3 One of these is very expensive. Which one is it?
a sugar b salt c herring
d flour e lobster

4 The credit card was invented in
a 1871 b 1914 c 1945
d 1950 e 1960

5 One of these is not in your bathroom. Which one is it?
a bath tub b soap c shower
d towel e sofa

6 One of these is not a vegetable. Which one is it?
a curly kail b lamb's lettuce c parsnips
d spinach e mango

7 One of these craftsmen (Handwerker) does not work with food. Who is it?
a baker b butcher c milkman
d grocer e chemist

8 The colour of a honeydew melon is
a yellow b white c black
d violet e green

9 One of these has nothing to do with whiskey. Which one is it?
a liquid b Scotland c distillery
d barley e Ireland

10 The favourite drink of the British is
a tea with lemon b tea with rum c tea with brandy
d tea with milk and sugar e tea with sour cream

11 One of these does not grow on a bush. Which one is it?
a peanut b redcurrant c blackcurrant
d raspberry e gooseberry

12 One of these is not in the kitchen. Which one?

a freezer | b microwave | c fridge
d dishwasher | e bedside table

13 Which of these does the butcher not sell?

a joint | b chop | c umbrella
d black pudding | e minced meat

14 The container large quantities of potatoes are sold in is a

a bottle | b bag | c jar
d box | e sack

15 A big white bird with a long neck many Germans eat at Christmas is the

a hen | b chicken | c goose
d duck | e turkey

16 Where would you have to go if you wanted to buy carnations?

a cheese counter | b florist | c baker
d butcher | e grocer

17 One of these does not live in Europe. Which one is it?

a pig | b hippo | c hare
d roe deer | e stag

18 Your colleague is away from work because she has a flu (Grippe). How would you say?

a she is on ill leave | b she is asleep | c she is on holiday
d she has some days off | e she is on sick leave

19 One of these is different from the others – it burns. Which one is it?

a Coke | b coke | c concrete
d rock | e stone

20 The capital of Northern Ireland is

a Dublin | b Edinburgh | c Belfast
d London | e Cardiff

4.3 Exercise Definitions

pound soup joint breakfast asparagus station personnel whale meat peel tin Spain purse credit card round Friday Labour Day aunt socket bakery

1 a container for food which is made from sheet metal *(Blech)*
2 what the dog likes to eat

3 the outside of an orange or apple
4 the day after Thursday
5 many customers pay with it instead of cash
6 454 grams are one
7 a white vegetable that grows in the ground
8 Liquid food we eat hot is
9 a container made of leather for money
10 A large piece of meat the butcher sells is a
11 the place where a train stops
12 After you got up in the morning, you usually eat
13 The biggest animal we know is the
14 The device in a room that gives electricity is the
15 the shape of coins
16 Sherry comes from
17 Your mother's sister is your
18 Another word for "staff" is
19 A shop where you can rolls is a
20 the 1st of May

4.4 Exercise Fill the gaps

Let me help you, please!

This was Michael's third day at the checkout and he .... *(langsam)* began to get used to the job, he even began to like it. So .... *(früh)* in the morning before the market opened, Michael .... *(melden)* to the checkout supervisor (today a young man named Adrian was doing the job because Susan had a day off) to collect the box with the change. He checked it and then took it to the checkout where he put it into the .... *(Schublade)* of the cash register. Then he tapped in his identification number to start the program. He also had to .... *(eingeben)* the amount of cash he had in the money drawer so that the system could always work out how much money he had in his cash register. He also needed that figure to .... *(abstimmen)* in the evening or whenever he had to hand the checkout over to another cashier. Michael made himself .... *(bequem)* in his chair and waited for the first customer to come. This was a lady with a trolley full of shopping which gave Michael a good .... *(Gelegenheit)* to practise his skills as a cashier. The lady paid by credit card, so he didn't have to handle any cash, it was a simple .... *(Verfahren)*. All he had to do was to pull the card through the card reader and wait for the system to clear the amount. He ....

(zurückgeben) the card to the customer and thanked her for doing her shopping in this particular market. The morning was fairly .... *(ruhig)* which gave Michael enough time to improve his skills. At 11 o'clock he was relieved by another colleague. He now had an hour off. It was time for a good .... *(Mittagessen)*. He rushed to the sandwich bar where he bought a cheese and onion sandwich and another one filled with crispy .... *(Frühstücksspeck)* and tomatoes. After he had taken over the check-out again after his lunch break, he .... *(plötzlich)* saw something very .... *(ungewöhnlich)*. A group of boys and girls in uniform turned up and positioned themselves at the ends of all the checkouts. What could this be? Fortunately Adrian, the checkout supervisor, ... *(stehen)* next to his checkout, so he asked him. "Oh yes, Michael, I forgot to tell you. It is Wednesday afternoon, and on Wednesdays the Scouts come here to work as packers for the customers. These here are Wolf Cubs and Brownies, young boys and girls who wish to .... *(werden)* Boy Scouts and Girl Guides. They help our customers to pack all their shopping into .... *(Plastiktüten)*, and they always get a .... *(einige wenige)* pence for their help which they .... *(sammeln)* for their annual summer camp. The customers like them, so we let them do it." After a short time, the Scouts eagerly began to help the customers at the checkouts, the skilfully took all they stuff from the .... *(Laufband)* and put it in .... *(Plastiktüten)*, and they even helped customers with full trolleys to push them to the car park. Michael then did not have much time to watch the Scouts it slowly got very busy. Most people had finished work, and now they went shopping. At five o'clock, he was relieved by another cashier. He took the money box out of the .... *(Schublade)*, checked out at the terminal and took the box over to the supervisor's office. The supervisor already had Michael's .... *(Kassenbestand)* available (he has a special computer program for it), so they .... *(zählen)* the money in Michael's cashbox – and once again, he balanced straight away.

Unit 5

Section 1 Texts

Information, please

One of the first places you come to when you enter a big supermarket is the information desk, and this position has to be manned all the time. It is here where customers come to with all sorts of questions, and these questions must be answered in a friendly and competent way. That is why only very experienced personnel with a very good knowledge of the market and the products are allowed to work here, and this position is equipped with all the necessary electronic devices such as PC and bar code scanner. The information desk is the domain of Mrs Mildred Hesketh-Covington, an elderly lady. Her working experience is well above average, she had been with the company for more than thirty years. After Michael had been formally introduced to Mrs Hesketh (he already knew her because he had met her several times during his breaks in the social room of the market) he was told to come behind the counter. Suddenly his eyes fell on a large number of umbrellas nicely piled under the counter.
"Excuse me, Mrs Hesketh, but what are you doing with all these umbrellas here?" he asked.
"Oh yes, the umbrellas" she replied with a smile, "this is a new customer service we provide. It is our "Rent an umbrella" service. Customers can hire them against a small

deposit – we usually take a fiver. It happens that people enter the market when the sun is shining and when they are leaving it is raining. And then they need an umbrella because they left their own one in the car. Our English weather, you know. We often get unexpected showers, don't we?" David was amused.

The staff at the information desk not only have to give information, they also have to deal with complaints, and that again is a very difficult job. Michael now had gathered enough experience to help Mrs Hesketh-Covington. Remember, he had worked in nearly all the departments of the market now, and he had even worked as a cashier for several weeks. First, Michael thought that Mrs Hesketh was a little bit strict because she took her work very serious and no one in the market called her by her Christian name (unofficially she was called "Aunt Mildred", but only when she was not around), but he soon found that she was a very kind lady. She knew the answers to all questions customers asked, and she gave Michael excellent demonstrations of how to deal with difficult customers and make them happy. She never lost her temper or patience. Michael soon realised that he had never learnt so much in such a short time because Mrs Hesketh not only explained to him that things had to be done in certain ways but she also explained to him why they had to be done in these particular ways. After two or three days at the information desk, Michael felt confident enough to give information on his own, and he understood Mrs Hesketh's opinion quite well when she said that the tasks at the information desk are really manifold and that not everybody would be suitable for the job. Besides giving information to customers, there were other jobs which the staff at the information desk had to do. Twice a week new flyers with the special offers of the week were printed and distributed. Of course, the information desk always got a large pile of flyers which they gave to all the customers who asked for them. The company also publishes a series of cards with easy-to-cook recipes (a new one comes out every Monday), and quite a few customers come to collect them.

Vocabulary List

experience	Erfahrung
experienced	erfahren
staff/personnel	Belegschaft, Personal
average	Durchschnitt
umbrella	Regenschirm
explain (to, r)	erklären
provide (to, r)	bereitstellen
rent (to, r)	mieten
deposit	Pfand
a fiver	a banknote to the value of five pound sterling

shower	hier: Regenschauer
strict	streng
deal with (to)	sich um etwas kümmern
gather (to, r)	sammeln, zusammenbringen
temper	Laune
patience	Geduld
confident (adj)	zuversichtlich
opinion	Meinung, Auffassung
manifold	vielfach
recipe	Kochrezept

For the irregular verbs in this story which are all in the past tense please refer to the "ABC of irregular verbs" in the annex of this book.

Text 2 Another lesson learnt

Michael quickly got used to his new job at the information desk, and he found it most interesting. It was never boring, and there was no hard work such as lifting and carrying heavy crates and boxes involved. One morning, Mrs Hesketh went for her tea break and left Michael on his own because she was now sure that he could do the job without supervision.
As soon as she had gone, an old lady turned up. Obviously something had gone wrong because she did not return the smile he gave her. She seemed to be in a very bad mood.
"Good morning, madam. How can I help you?"
"Good morning to you, young man. I don't think you can help me, I would like to have word with the lady who usually works here. Is she not in today?
"Oh yes, of course Mrs Hesketh-Covington is in today. She will be back in a minute or so. But what is your problem?"
The lady took a carton of milk from her shopping basket and put it on the counter.
"See this carton of milk I bought yesterday? It smelled a bit funny when I opened it, and I think it is off. And would you believe, the sell-by date has also expired!"
Michael took the carton and looked at the sell-by date. It had indeed expired. But this was hardly possible. The manager and all the staff in the dairy products department check fresh and perishable products such as milk every morning in order to make sure that no expired items at all are left on the shelves.
"Excuse me, madam, but do you have the receipt for the milk?
"No, young man, I don't. What a silly question. Do you think I keep all my receipts – just in case?"

This moment, Mrs Hesketh-Covington returned from her tea break and she immediately took over.
30 "Ah, good morning Mrs Grouch. What is your problem today?"
"See this carton of milk? It is off, and I bought it yesterday!"
Mrs Hesketh did not hesitate at all, she did not even look at the expiry date on the carton. She asked Michael to take the milk carton, dispose of it and bring Mrs Grouch a carton of fresh milk from the dairy products department which she gave to the old lady after he had
35 returned.
"There you are, Mrs Grouch, we are terribly sorry that you had a problem with one of our products. But now I think everything is fine, you now have fresh milk."
Mrs Grouch thanked for the help and walked off, pulling her trolley with her shopping basket behind her. As soon as Mrs Grouch had left, Mrs Hesketh turned to Michael and
40 explained to him:
"Poor Mrs Grouch is a little bit forgetful. She must have left this milk in her fridge for ages, I think she simply forgot it. But this is part of our customer service. We do not argue in such a situation, we simply replace the item, and we even apologize for mistakes we have not made." Michael was impressed. This is the right way to make and keep satisfied
45 customers. Another lesson learnt.

Vocabulary List

bad mood	schlechte Laune
to have word with s.o.	mit jemanden sprechen
sell-by date	Verfallsdatum
expire	ablaufen, ungültig werden
receipt	Kassenzettel, Quittung
grouch (the)	Nörgler, Miesepeter
argue (to, r)	sich streiten
perishable	leicht verderblich
dispose (to, r) of s.th.	etwas entsorgen
hesitate (to, r)	zögern
apologize	entschuldigen
satisfied (to be)	zufrieden

For the irregular verbs in this story which are all in the past tense please refer to the "ABC of irregular verbs" in the annex of this book.

Comprehension exercise

Please answer the following questions in full sentences.

1 Describe the basic equipment of a good information desk.
2 What are the umbrellas used for?
3 How can customers get an umbrella when it rains?

4 Why did Michael learn so much at the information desk?
5 Which other services do they provide at this particular information desk?
6 Why did the customer (Mrs Grouch) complain?
7 What did Michael try to do first?
8 How did Mrs Hesketh solve the problem?
9 How exactly did she apologize?
10 What is the company policy in case of complaints?

Section 2 Basics

2.1 Nations & nationalities

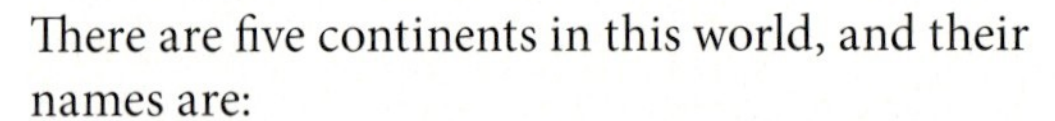

Note

All words on these lists must be written with capital letters

There are five continents in this world, and their names are:
Europe, Africa, Asia, America and Australia
Some of the most important European countries:

country	adjective	the language spoken in this country	inhabitant	EU-member
Germany	German	German	German	yes
France	French	French	Frenchman/ Frenchwoman	yes
Belgium	Belgian	German, French, Dutch	Belgian	yes
The Netherlands	Dutch	Dutch	Dutchman	yes
Luxembourg	Luxembour-gian	French, German	Luxembourger	yes
Denmark	Danish	Danish	Dane	yes
Norway	Norwegian	Norwegian	Norwegian	no
Sweden	Swedish	Swedish	Swede	yes
Finland	Finnish	Finnish	Finn	yes

country	adjective	the language spoken in this country	inhabitant	EU-member
United Kingdom	British	English	Brit/Briton	yes
(England)	English	English	Englishman/ Englishwoman	
(Wales)	Welsh	English/Welsh	Welshman/ Welshwoman	
(Scotland)	Scottish/Scotch	English	Scotsman/ Scotswoman	
(Northern Ireland) Irish	English	Irishman/ Irishwoman		
Republic of Ireland	Irish	English/Gaelic	Irishman/ Irishwoman	yes
Spain	Spanish	Spanish	Spaniard	yes
Portugal	Portuguese	Portuguese	Portuguese	yes
Switzerland	Swiss	German, French, Italian	Swiss	no
Austria	Austrian	German	Austrian	yes
Italy	Italian	Italian	Italian	yes
Hungary	Hungarian	Hungarian	Hungarian	yes
Greece	Greek	Greek	Greek	yes
Cyprus	Cyprian	Greek/Turkish	Cyprian	yes
Turkey	Turkish	Turkish	Turk	no
Czech Republic	Czech	Czech	Czech	yes
Poland	Polish	Polish	Pole	yes
Russia	Russian	Russian	Russian	no
Estonia	Estonian	Estonian	Estonian	yes
Latvia	Latvian	Latvian	Latvian	yes
Lithuania	Lithuanian	Lithuanian	Lithuanina	yes
Romania	Romanian	Romanian	Romanian	yes
Bulgaria	Bulgarian	Bulgarian	Bulgarian	yes

country	adjective	the language spoken in this country	inhabitant	EU-member
Slovakia	Slovakian	Slovakian	Slovak	yes
Slovenia	Slovenian	Slovenian	Slovenian	yes
Malta	Maltese	Maltese	Maltese	yes
American countries				
United States	American	English	American	
Canada	Canadian	English, French	Canadian	
Mexico	Mexican	Spanish	Mexican	
Brazil	Brazilian	Portuguese	Brazilian	
Argentina	Argentinian	Spanish	Argentinian	
Other countries and continents				
Africa	African	*	African	
Asia	Asian	*	Asian	
India	Indian	*	Indian	
Japan	Japanese	Japanese	Japanese	
China	Chinese	*	Chinese	
Korea	Korean	Korean	Korean	
Australia	Australian	English	Australian	
New Zealand	New Zealand	English	New Zealander	

** This is a continent with many nations and many national languages or a country where many different languages are spoken.*

Exercise NATIONS AND NATIONALITIES

Note

Important: All words on these lists must be written with capital letters.

1 There are five continents in this world, and their names are:
2 Some of the most important countries:

	English name of the country	adjective	language spoken in this country
Deutschland			
Frankreich			
Niederlande			
Dänemark			
Norwegen			
Schweden			
Finnland			
Vereinigtes Königreich			
England			
Wales			
Schottland			
Irland			
Spanien			
Portugal			
Schweiz			
Österreich			
Italien			
Ungarn			
Griechenland			
Türkei			
Tschechien			
Polen			
Russland			
Rumänien			
Bulgarien			
USA			
Kanada			
Brasilien			
China			
Japan			
Australien			
Indien			
China			
Korea			
Afrika			

Exercise FOREIGN COUNTRIES AND THEIR CAPITALS

Please write down the English name of the following countries and their appropriate capitals. The list below may help you.

Brussels Canberra Stockholm Berlin Warsaw Madrid aris Brasilia Berne The Hague Ankara Tokyo London Vienna Athens Moscow Rome Ottawa Prague Oslo Copenhagen Washington D.C.

	English name	**capital**
Deutschland		
Frankreich		
Belgien		
Niederlande		
Vereinigtes Königreich		
Schweiz		
Österreich		
Italien		
Spanien		
Dänemark		
Norwegen		
Schweden		
Russland		
Tschechische Republik		
Griechenland		
Türkei		
Polen		
Japan		
Vereinigte Staaten		
Brasilien		
Australien		
Kanada		

Exercise

Example:

This apple comes from Germany. It is a .... apple
This apple comes from Germany. It is a German apple.

And now it is your turn:

1 These Brussels sprouts come from Belgium. They are .... Brussels sprouts.

2 This pineapple comes from Africa. It is an .... pineapple.

3 These noodles come from Italy. They are .... noodles.

4 This fish comes from Norway. It is .... fish.

5 This cheese comes from France. It is .... cheese.

6 This chocolate comes from Switzerland. It is .... chocolate.

7 These toffees come from Scotland. They are .... toffees.

8 These tomatoes come from The Netherlands. They are .... tomatoes.

9 This lamb comes from Australia. It is .... lamb.

10 This salami comes from Hungary. It is .... salami.

11 This red wine comes from Spain. It is .... red wine.

12 These oranges come from Greece. They are .... oranges.

13 This lobster is from Canada. It is a .... lobster.

14 This bottle of vodka is from Russia. It is .... vodka.

15 This coffee comes from Brazil. It is .... coffee.

16 This tea comes from India. It is .... tea.

2.2 Useful phrases *Nützliche Redewendungen*

Begrüßung:
Good morning
Guten Morgen (bis 12.00 Uhr)

Good afternoon
Guten Tag (eigentlich: Guten Nachmittag bis ca. 18.00 Uhr)

Good evening
Guten Abend (ab ca. 18.00 Uhr)

Good night
Gute Nacht (am späteren Abend zum Abschied)

Sehr oft hört man nach einer Begrüßung auch noch die Floskel "How are you today?".
Diese Frage ist aber nicht ernst gemeint, es ist eine reine Höflichkeitsfloskel, und deswegen

ist die übliche Antwort "Thank you, I'm fine – how are you?", wobei die Betonung deutlich auf dem "you" liegt.

Deutlich ältere weibliche Kunden werden selbstverständlich mit "madam" angeredet, für männliche Kunden gilt entsprechend die Anrede "sir". Dieselbe Regel gilt für Vorgesetzte.

Wenn wir Kunden nach ihren Wünschen fragen, dann ist unsere wichtigste Redewendung:

"Would you like to...?" *„Möchten Sie ...?"*

Wenn wir eine negative Antwort geben müssen, dann beginnen wir unseren Satz mit:

"I am sorry, but ..." *„Es tut mit leid, aber ..."*

"I beg your pardon" *„Ich bitte um Entschuldigung"*

Wichtige andere Redewendungen:

How can I help you?
Wie kann ich Ihnen helfen?

Do you need help?
Brauchen Sie Hilfe?

Please follow me!
Bitte folgen Sie mir!

What are you looking for?
Was suchen Sie?

Are you looking for anything in particular?
Suchen Sie etwas Bestimmtes?

Please follow me, I will show you where to find it.
Bitte folgen Sie mir, ich zeigen Ihnen, wo es ist.

Yes, this item is on special offer this week.
Ja, diesen Artikel haben wir diese Woche im Sonderangebot.

Sorry, but this item is not on special offer this week.
Es tut mir leid, aber diesen Artikel haben wir diese Woche nicht im Sonderangebot.

Sorry, this item is not in stock at the moment.
Es tut mir leid, diesen Artikel haben wir im Moment nicht vorrätig.

Shall I order it for you?
Soll ich das für Sie bestellen?

Yes I can recommend it.
Ja, das kann ich Ihnen empfehlen.

No, I cannot recommend it.
Nein, das kann ich Ihnen nicht empfehlen.

Just a moment please, I will call my colleague.
Einen Moment bitte, ich werde meinen Kollegen/meine Kollegin rufen.

Just a moment please, I will call the responsible person.
Einen Moment bitte, ich werde die verantwortliche Person rufen.

What is your problem?
Was für ein Problem haben Sie?

I am sure we can solve your problem.
Ich bin sicher dass wir Ihr Problem lösen können

Of course we will replace the faulty item.
Natürlich werden wir das fehlerhafte Produkt ersetzen.

How would you like to pay?
Wie möchten Sie bezahlen?

Shall I wrap it for you?
Soll ich es Ihnen einpacken/einwickeln?

Would you like to have a carrier bag?
Möchten Sie eine Plastiktüte haben?

It will be weighed at the checkout.
Es wird an der Kasse gewogen.

The article/item you are looking for is on the shelf at the end of the aisle.
Der Artikel den Sie suchen ist im Regal am Ende des Ganges.

Yes, there is a deposit on the bottle.
Ja, auf der Flasche ist Pfand.

No, there is no deposit on the bottle.
Nein, auf der Flasche ist kein Pfand.

Shall I call a taxi for you?
Soll ich Ihnen ein Taxi rufen?

I am sorry, but this credit card is not valid.
Es tut mir leid, aber diese Kreditkarte ist ungültig

I am sorry, but this banknote is a forgery. I am not allowed to return it.
Es tut mir leid, aber diese Banknote ist falsch. Ich darf sie nicht zurückgeben.

Follow the main aisle until you come to a …, then turn left/right.
Gehen Sie den Hauptgang entlang, bis Sie zu … kommen, dort nach links/rechts gehen.

Just a moment please.
Einen Moment bitte.

Just a moment, I will find out how much it costs.
Einen Moment, ich werde herausfinden, was es kostet.

Would you like to exchange it?
Möchten Sie das umtauschen?

Do you have the receipt?
Haben Sie den Kassenzettel?

Just a moment. I will call the manager.
Einen Moment, ich werde den Marktleiter rufen.

> **Note**
> Und immer daran denken: Wenn sich jemand mit "thank you" o.ä. bedankt, dann sagt man "You are welcome" – das entspricht unserem „Bitte sehr/Gern geschehen“

2.3 Problems with the storage of food

Most foodstuffs can only be stored for a limited period of time, and some of them only for a very limited period. This period of time is called the shelf life. On the label of English foodstuffs it usually says "best before ...". A good example for a foodstuff with a very short shelf life is milk. It will turn sour after it has reached the end of its shelf life. When milk is sour, it does not smell good, we say that the milk is "off". It would not be dangerous to drink milk that is off, it would simply be not very pleasant because of the smell and the taste. But other foodstuffs can be dangerous when they are too old, when they have been stored incorrectly, when the instructions for hygiene have not been followed correctly or when something else is wrong with them. Here are some examples:

ant	often on vegetables and fruits that grew near the ground, disgusting but harmless
botulinum toxid ☠	a very powerful and therefore highly dangerous toxic (poison) that causes botulism which can be fatal. Usually found in tinned food (e.g. meat, beans) a warning sign for the presence of botulinum toxic is the rounded (convex) top of a tin. There will be a hissing sound when you open such a tin.
caterpillar	usually the grub of the cabbage white butterfly, often found on cauliflower and cabbage, is disgusting but harmless
cockroach	often found in rooms where food is stored or prepared, disgusting but relatively harmless
earwig	often found on vegetables, harmless
fly	a health hazard, flies may transfer infections of all kinds
fruit fly	as the name implies, a small fly living on all kinds of fruits, lays eggs which become small maggots or worms(e.g. in apples, cherries, raspberries, plums etc.), is disgusting but harmless
maggot	the grub of a fly, can live in a large variety of foodstuffs, is disgusting but harmless
mealworm	grub of the meal beetle, lives in flour, disgusting but harmless
mould	grows on decaying matter in different colours, is a severe health hazard, it is not sufficient to remove the infested part of the foodstuff

nematode	small worms that live in fish, a severe health hazard
rot	mainly on fruit and vegetables, they are decaying, rot is disgusting
salmonella poisoning	bacteria mainly living in poultry and eggs, grow rapidly when the foodstuff is not kept cool, a severe health hazard
slug	a kind of snail with no house, often lives on lettuce, is disgusting but harmless
trichina	small worms living in pork, a severe health hazard
wasp	often fly around bakery produce, are no health hazard as such but may sting

Vocabulary List

foodstuff	das einzelne Lebensmittel
shelf life	Haltbarkeit
decay	verwesen
ant	Ameise
fatal	tödlich
hissing sound	Zischen
cockroach	Kakerlake
earwig	Ohrenkneifer, Ohrwurm
caterpillar	Raupe
grub	Larve
cabbage white butterfly	Kohlweißling (Schmetterling)
disgusting	widerlich, ekelhaft
fly	Fliege
transfer (to, r)	übertragen
fruit fly	Fruchtfliege
maggot	Made
worm	Wurm
meal worm	Mehlwurm
mould	Schimmel
infested	befallen
health hazard	Gesundheitsgefahr
rot	Fäulnis
slug	Nacktschnecke
wasp	Wespe
sting (to, ir)	stechen

Section 3 Brush up your grammar

3.1 The modal "must" — *Das Hilfsverb "must"*

Vorsicht ist beim Gebrauch des englischen Wortes "must" geboten (siehe auch Lektion 2, Abschnitt 2.2.4 "On the little word "must"). Dieses Wort hat keinesfalls dieselbe Bedeutung wie unser deutsches Wort „müssen“, es ist erheblich schärfer. In der deutschen Sprache wird das Wort „müssen“ unbefangen verwendet, so sagen wir zu einem Kunden: „Dann müssen Sie dort im dritten Regal schauen“.

In der englischen Sprache dagegen steckt hinter dem Wort "must" immer eine Drohung, das heißt, es ist mit Folgen bzw. Konsequenzen zu rechnen, wenn die mit "must" formulierte Aufforderung nicht befolgt wird.

Daher sollten wir das Wort „müssen“ in der englischen Sprache besser durch "have to" (Beispiel: "You have to go to the fresh meat counter) ersetzen. Ausnahmen bei der Verwendung gibt es, wenn Gefahr besteht. Beispiel: "You must leave the market immediately!" (z. B. beim Ausbruch eines Feuers). Für sich selbst kann man das Wort "must" natürlich verwenden, da man selber entscheiden kann, ob es angebracht ist. Beispiel: "I must go now". Das ist meine eigene Entscheidung und niemand anders wird unter Druck gesetzt.

Das Wort "must" kann man nur im "present tense" (Gegenwart) verwenden, im "simple past" (Vergangenheit) heißt es dann immer "had to".

Zudem hat das Modalverb "must" noch zwei verschiedene negative Formen mit unterschiedlichen Bedeutungen:

Beispiele: You must not drink and drive. It is dangerous. *(verboten)*
You need not do the washing up. We have a dish washer. *(unnötig)*

Negative Form	Bedeutung	
Michael must not miss his bus to school.	It is necessary or important for Michael to catch his bus, because if he does not catch the bus, he will be too late at work. If he is late at work, his managers are angry. His bosses do not allow him to be late.	must not *(darf nicht)*
Michael need not get up early today.	There is no work today so it is not important to get up early. He may stay in bed a bit longer.	need not *(braucht nicht)*

EXERCISE:

Make questions and negations.

Beispiel:
We must do our homework.
q Must we do our homework?
n We need not do our homework on Sunday.

1 Michael’ father must work from 9 to 5 o’clock.
q
n at the weekend.

2 The cleaner must sweep the floors.

q

n brush shoes.

3 Michael's mother must take the underground to work.

q

n if her husband takes her to work.

3.2 Prepositions *Präpositionen*

Präpositionen sagen uns, wo oder wann etwas geschieht. Da es aber in der englischen Sprache für viele Präpositionen keine Regeln gibt, kann man sie am besten im Zusammenhang mit einem kurzen Satz lernen.
Hier sind einige Grundregeln:

Wochentage (Monday etc.)	on
Zeiträume (morning, afternoon etc.)	in
Zeitpunkte (einschl. Uhrzeiten)	at
Orte	at
wenn über etwas gesprochen wird	about
wenn etwas geschrieben steht	on
wenn etwas aus etwas gemacht ist	of
wenn man sich um etwas kümmert	with
wenn mit etwas Handel getrieben wird	in
Termine, Fristen	by
durchgehende Tätigkeit etc. bis	until

Häufig gemachte Fehler
Grundsätzlich sollte man beachten, dass die Anwendung von Präpositionen im Deutschen und Englischen unterschiedlich ist, man kann sie fast nie wörtlich übersetzen. Eine der wenigen Ausnahmen ist die Ecke im Zimmer, hier heißt es sowohl im Deutschen als auch im Englischen "in der Ecke = in the corner".
Aber: Wenn ein Haus an der Ecke steht, dann ist es das Haus "on the corner", und wenn wir uns an der Ecke treffen wollen, dann heißt es "at the corner".

Ein häufig gemachter Fehler ist die Verwendung der Präposition im Zusammenhang mit Handeltreiben. Hier muss es heißen: "to deal in s.th."
Wenn wir uns aber um etwas kümmern, dann heißt es "to deal with".

Zu beachten ist auch die für die Lagerhaltung verwendete Präposition. Hier heißt es "in stock", wenn wir etwas am Lager haben, und wir müssen "from stock" sagen, wenn wir etwas ab Lager liefern.

Wenn wir über etwas sprechen, dann verwendet man die Präposition "about". Für Geschriebenes gilt aber unbedingt "on", also "a book on horses","a newspaper article" on the financial crisis" etc.

Wenn ich mit jemanden spreche, dann heißt das "to talk to someone".

Wenn man auf einem Stuhl sitzt, dann sitzt man "in the chair".
Verben können durch Präpositionen ihren Sinn ändern werden. Ein gutes Beispiel dafür ist das Verb "to look".

Beispiele:	to look after	=	aufpassen
	to look for	=	suchen
	to look at	=	ansehen
	to look up	=	etwas nachschlagen (Wörterbuch, Telefonbuch etc.)
	to look away	=	den Blick abwenden
	to look like	=	aussehen wie
	to look onto	=	auf etwas blicken

Exercise

And now it is your turn: Put in the right prepositions.

1 The information desk team .... our supermarket consists .... 3 members.

2 I do not like to talk .... my neighbour, she is very unfriendly.

3 His mother told him to look .... his little sister. *(aufpassen)*

4 I met him .... the station, not .... the waiting room.

5 I met him .... the entrance of the cinema, not .... it. *(vor dem Kino, nicht darin)*

6 Yes, we have the item .... stock, so we can deliver .... stock. *(item = Ding, Gegenstand, Sache)*

7 Everything in this company is .... control.

8 The television set .... the corner there is not new.

9 Tables and chairs are usually made .... wood.

10 I work .... the personnel department .... a big international chain of supermarkets.

11 In the house .... the corner is a very nice shop.

12 The boy looked .... his guinea pig all afternoon. *(suchen)*

13 Here is an urgent order .... 500 bottles of French red wine, but we have to increase the price per unit .... 8 percent.

14 I am talking to you .... behalf of the manager. (im Auftrag von)

15 This is a book .... accounting, but I am not interested .... this subject.

16 I don't want to talk .... that right now.

17 In this shop, we deal .... bicycles and accessories. *(Handel treiben mit ....)*

18 I told him to come .... the afternoon, not .... noon.

19 The doctor asked me to see him .... Monday .... three o'clock .... his surgery. *(surgery = Arztpraxis)*

20 I deal .... all the things my boss is too busy to do. *(sich um etwas kümmern)*

21 In this town, all pubs close .... midnight.

22 This book has to be returned .... Friday. *(Rückgabefrist)*

23 His mother told him to look .... his little brother.

24 I don't know their telephone number, I have to look it .... in the phone book.

25 Come quick, the CEO is .... the phone!

26 Look at this photo, you can see my dog .... it.

27 This week, I have to work .... until Friday. *(durchgehend bis Freitag arbeiten)*

Section 4 Practise your word power

4.1 Exercise Word groups

Put each of the words below into the correct list. *Use each word only once!*
Can you think of more words to add to each list?

brush shower gel biro banknote customer knife napkins broom toothpaste purse cashier duster whisk paperclip bucket conveyor band change rubber gravy ladle toothbrush coin scanner dustpan credit card pencil toilet paper corkscrew sponge trolley writing pad ruler to pay bottle opener plastic bag tin opener washing-up liquid

1 At the checkout

....
....
....
....
....
....

2 Money

....
....
....
....
....
....

3 Cleaning

....

....

....

....

....

....

4 Stationery

....

....

....

....

....

....

5 Household utensils

....

....

....

....

....

....

6 Chemistry

....

....

....

....

....

....

4.2 Exercise Odd man out

Only one answer is right. Which one is it?

1 What is the right order of size (beginning with the smallest)?
   a pumpkin, cherry, plum, apple, pea
   b pea, cherry, plum, apple, pumpkin
   c cherry, pumpkin, apple, pea, plum
   d apple, pea, plum, cherry, pumpkin
   e plum, apple, pumpkin, pea, cherry

2 One of these lives in the water. Which one?
   a swan   b herring   c duck
   d goose   e stork

3 One of these is wrong. Which one is it?
   a The customer buys some cheese.
   b The customers buys some cheese.
   c The customer bought some cheese.
   d The customers bought some cheese.
   e The customer will buy some cheese.

4 Rum is made from
a sugar cane b milk c hops and malt
d fruit e wheat

5 One of these vegetables is typical for winter. Which one is it?
a asparagus b lettuce c garden-fresh peas
d cauliflower e Brussels sprouts

6 One of the words in the plural is wrong. Which one?
a cabbages b shelves c fishes
d sheep e roofs

7 What is the correct abbreviation for "circa, ungefähr"?
a e.g. b i.e c approx.
d wef e asap

8 The colour of liquorice is
a blue b white c black
d violet e green

9 One of these has nothing to do with wine. Which one is it?
a liquid b grapes c vineyard
d barley e dry

10 The British national flag is called the
a Union Jack b Union John c Union James
d Union James e Union George

11 One of these grows in water. Which one is it?
a corn b wheat c oats
d barley e rice

12 Which one is the fastest?
a lorry b van c forklift
d car e tractor

13 Which of these becomes sweet when it is frozen?
a water b kail c Brussels sprouts
d lamb's lettuce e potatoes

14 Which of these animals has no horns?

a buffalo	b cow	c goat
d sow	e ram	

15 Which of these does not lay eggs?

a hen	b goose	c ladybird
d duck	e turkey	

16 Which of these does a butcher not sell?

a mince	b mint	c joint
d ham	e chop	

17 All these are fish. One lives in saltwater and also in freshwater. Which one is it?

a trout	b shark	c carp
d salmon	e herring	

18 Which of these things is soft?

a broom	b bucket	c dustpan
d sponge	e brush	

19 The part of your body between your head and your chest is your

a elbow	b belly	c neck
d back	e thigh	

20 The English name of the "Ostsee" is

a East Sea	b Baltic Sea	c Atlantic Ocean
d Lake Constance	e Mediterranean Sea	

4.3 Exercise Definitions

gallon Tuesday bone toilet plum
pair of scissors abbreviation coconut mice May
banana year clock trailer hangover
flour Christmas Eve cousin leather haberdashery

1 a long yellow fruit (slightly bent) which we eat raw
2 what the cat likes to eat
3 Labour Day is always in the month of
4 annually means once a
5 the vehicle (it has no engine) pulled by a lorry
6 In Britain, 4.5 litres are a
7 a blue or yellow fruit that grows on trees
8 the third day after Good Friday is
9 the device on the wall that shows the time
10 the part of the chop you cannot eat
11 the place where customers go to if they have to follow a call of nature
12 This is what you need if you want to cut paper
13 The biggest nut we know is the
14 Ground cereals are called
15 This is what you have in the morning if you drink too much alcohol
16 Wallets and purses are made of
17 Your uncle's son is your
18 A long word made short is an
19 A shop where you can buy zips and buttons is a
20 The 24th of December is

4.4 Exercise Fill the gaps

Information, please

One of the first places you come to when you .... *(betreten, eintreten)* a big supermarket is the information desk, and this position has to be manned all the time. It is here where customers come to with all sorts of questions, and these questions must be answered in a .... *(freundlich)* and competent way. That is why only very .... *(erfahren)* personnel with a very good knowledge of the market and the products are allowed to work here, and this position was equipped with all the .... *(notwendig)* electronic .... *(Geräte)* such as PC and bar code scanner. The information desk was the domain of Mrs Mildred Hesketh-Covington, an elderly lady. Her working experience was well above .... *(Durchschnitt)*, she had been with the company for more than thirty years. After Michael had been formally introduced to Mrs

Hesketh (he .... *(schon)* knew her because he had met her several times during his .... *(Pausen)* in the social room of the market) he was told to come behind the counter. Suddenly his eyes fell on a large number of umbrellas nicely piled under the counter.

"Excuse me, Mrs Hesketh, but what are you doing with all these umbrellas here?" he asked. "Oh yes, the umbrellas" she replied with a smile, "this is a new customer service we provide. It is our "Rent an umbrella" service. Customers can .... *(mieten)* them against a small .... *(Pfand)* – we usually take a fiver. It happens that people enter the market when the sun is shining, and when they are leaving it is raining. And then they need an umbrella because they left their own one in the car. Our English weather, you know. We often get unexpected .... *(Schauer)*, don't we?" David was amused.

The staff at the information desk not only have to give information, they also have to deal with .... *(Beschwerden)*, and that again is a very difficult job. Michael now had gathered .... *(genug)* experience to help Mrs Hesketh-Covington. Remember, he had worked in nearly all the departments of the market now, and he had even worked as a .... *(Kassierer)* for several weeks. First, Michael thought that Mrs Hesketh was a little bit strict because she took her work very .... *(ernst)* and no one in the market called her by her Christian name (unofficially she was called "Aunt Mildred", but only when she was not around), but he soon found that she was a very kind lady. She knew the answers to all questions customers asked, and she gave Michael .... *(ausgezeichnet)* demonstrations of how to deal with difficult customers and make them happy. She never lost her temper or .... *(Geduld)*. Michael soon realised that he had never learnt so much in such a short time because Mrs Hesketh not only .... *(erklären)* to him that things had to be done in certain ways but she also explained to him why they had to be done in these particular ways. After two or three days at the information desk, Michael felt confident .... *(genug)* to give information on his own, and he understood Mrs Hesketh's opinion quite well when she said that the .... *(Aufgaben)* at the information desk are really manifold and that not .... *(jedermann)* would be .... *(geeignet)* for the job. Besides giving information to customers, there were other jobs which the staff at the information desk had to do. Twice a week new .... *(Flugblätter)* with the special offers of the week were printed and distributed. Of course, the information desk always got a large pile of .... *(Flugblätter)* which they gave to all the customers who asked for them. The company also publishes a series of cards with easy-to-cook .... (Kochrezepte) (a new one comes out every Monday), and quite a few customers come to collect them.

Unit 6

Section 1 Texts

Text 1 Business before pleasure

On several occasions, Michael had to work overtime. That is why Sharon called him into her office one morning and asked him to take some days off as a compensation for the overtime he had worked. Michael was delighted, because he also had the weekend off, and that meant that he could go on nearly a week's holiday. London! In the afternoon, he called his friend Gordon who lives and works in London. Gordon was not at home this time of the day, quite obviously he had to work. So Michael left a message for Gordon on the answer phone and asked him to call him back in the evening. Some time later, Michael's telephone rang. He took off the receiver: Gordon was on the phone. Now Michael told Gordon that he would have the weekend and a few extra days off and that he would very much like to spend a few days in London, and he also would like to meet Gordon. Gordon immediately asked Michael to stay with him since he has a small flat in Knightsbridge (a district of London) not too far away from the world-famous department store of Harrods. Michael was glad that Gordon asked him to stay with him because accommodation in London is very expensive. They arranged to meet in the famous pub "The Sherlock" near Trafalgar Square in Westminster in central London. So Friday afternoon after work Michael took his holdall which he had packed the evening before (the usual things you need when travelling – pyjamas, toothbrush, charger for the mobile phone etc.), said "goodbye" to his workmates, left the supermarket and then headed for the station. The railway station was only a few minutes walk away from his workplace, and he did not have to wait long for a train to London Waterloo. Michael had bought a small used car some weeks ago, but he did not want to drive into central London. There is very much traffic there, it is expensive to drive into the city (the fee is £5 a day), and parking is nearly impossible. After he had arrived at Waterloo Station, he took the underground to Charing Cross. The pub they were going to meet in was

not far away from this underground station, so he could walk there. His friend Gordon was
25 already there and gave him a very friendly welcome. Now they walked to the bar and both called a pint, Gordon ordered a Guinness while Michael preferred a pint of best bitter. They got their beers and had to pay straight away which is normal practise in every British pub. Luckily enough, they found a small table where they could sit down and talk, Michael had so many questions to ask about Gordon's job, and Gordon liked to talk about his job. He
30 works in a big department store in Oxford Street, the main shopping street in London. The name of the store is Clearwoods & Sons. There are quite a few big department stores in Oxford Street such as Littlewoods, Debenhams and Marks & Spencer, and of course there are many other shops. First of all, Gordon gave Michael a plan of the layout of his department store so Michael could see how many departments the store has. Michael immedi-
35 ately noticed that the range of products differed considerably from the one in his own supermarket where the main emphasis is put on food. Gordon's store also has a food department, but it is mainly for delicatessen, exotic food and luxury food, not so much for the things you need for everyday life. After a while, Gordon interrupted their conversation: "I am quite hungry, I have not had a real meal all day. The bar food in here is very good, I
40 will go and get a quick nosh. What about you, Michael, shall I get you something to eat, too? You are my guest tonight!" Michael was delighted to hear that, he was hungry too. "Thank you Gordon, that is very kind of you!" They both looked at the blackboard on the wall where all the meals were written down with chalk. Gordon decided to take fish and chips, while Michael wanted a steak and kidney pie. Now Gordon went to the bar and
45 ordered the food. The barmaid took his order which he had to pay for straight away. Then he was given two tickets with numbers on. After a while, the girl came out of the kitchen with two plates in her hands, she called the numbers on their tickets. Gordon rushed to the bar to fetch the plates, and he brought cutlery and a salt cellar with him as well. Now they could enjoy their meals.

Vocabulary List

business before pleasure	(Sprichwort) Erst die Arbeit, dann das Vergnügen
occasion	Gelegenheit
compensation	Ausgleich
answer phone	Anrufbeantworter
ring (to, ir)	klingeln
receiver	Telephonhörer
flat	Wohnung/Mietwohnung
holdall	Reisetasche
charger	Ladegerät
fee	Gebühr
pint	Pinte, altes Hohlmass für Bier und Milch (1/8 Gallone, ca. 0,56 l) wird aber auch nach der Umstellung auf metrische Maße noch weiter verwendet
bitter	englische Biersorte, entspricht ungefähr unserem Altbier
emphasis	Schwerpunkt

nosh (U)	Essen
cutlery	Essbesteck
salt cellar	Salzstreuer

For the irregular verbs in this story which are all in the past tense please refer to the "ABC of irregular verbs" in the annex of this book.

Text 2 Oxford Street – shopper's paradise in central London

As mentioned before, Michael was very interested in Gordon's work. So after their meal he again listened carefully to what Gordon told him, and he only interrupted him every now and then to ask some additional questions. Gordon told him everything about his job in the very big and exclusive department store in Oxford Street where he works in the men's sportswear department and sells tennis rackets. This is the ideal job for him because he is a keen sportsman, his favourite sport, of course, is tennis. Clearwoods & Sons in Oxford Street is in a very big building with seven storeys, and there are some 50 departments and sub-departments in it. Now Gordon tried to explain to Michael how many departments there are in the store in Oxford Street, but he could not manage, there are simply too many. There are of course the usual ones such as a large food hall in the basement and large departments for household appliances (e.g. freezers, fridges, washing machines and tumble dryers), audivisual equipment (TVs, radios, DVD-players etc.), a large computer department, but also a very exclusive gift department, a perfume department (very exclusive and expensive), an even more exclusive department for watches and jewellery, a department for dinnerware, glassware and silverware (also quite exclusive) and, of course, a large toy department. Michael wanted to know how many different items they usually had in stock, but Gordon did not know, he simply said "Sorry, mate, it is an awful lot, that's all I know. But I tell you what – come and look yourself. You will still be here on Monday, just come in and see me in my department. I am sure I will be given the time to show you around for an hour or so." Michael did not hesitate to promise that he would come.

Later on that evening, Gordon's friend Gerry turned up and joined the two. Gordon had sent him an SMS that they would be in "The Sherlock" all evening. Gerry lives in Lambeth on the other side of the River Thames, and he works in a big D.I.Y. superstore in Hammersmith.

Now Michael could also learn a few things about a D.I.Y. store and what the work in such a store is like. He eagerly began to ask questions, and Gerry patiently tried to answer them all.

Most Britons have a house, and nearly every house in the U.K. has a garden. That is why gardening is the hobby of millions of people in the U.K., and for this hobby they require a
35 large number of tools (spade, hoe, rake, lawn mower, fertilizer, seeds etc.), plants and other things. The idea of D.I.Y. stores is not that old: The first ones appeared some 30 years ago, but now they are extremely popular, not only in the U.K. Besides gardening, more and more people do most of the repairs in their houses and flats themselves, and quite a few even do major jobs such as rebuilding a bathroom which requires a lot of special tools and
40 other equipment. The store Gerry works in is one of the biggest in London, and so Gerry explained to Michael the range of products such a store usually stocks: basic building materials (bricks, cement) including covering materials and insulating materials, tiles, lamps, bulbs, cables and fuses, wood and wood-based materials, all sorts of tools and power tools, paints and wallpapers, bathroom installations, everything you need for
45 gardening including tools and plants, special clothing, tools and materials for car maintenance and repair, tools and materials for bicycle maintenance and repair, to mention only a few. Gerry told Michael that they stock approx. 100.000 different items in his store. Michael was deeply impressed – four times as much as in his own supermarket.

Vocabulary List

racket	Tennisschläger
keen	eifrig, begeistert
jewellery	Juwelen, Schmuck
mate (U)	Kumpel, Freund
hesitate (to, r)	zögern
turn up (to, r)	auftauchen
D.I.Y. = do it yourself	selbermachen
D.I.Y. store	Baumarkt
spade	Spaten
hoe	hacke
rake	Rechen, Harke
lawn mower	Rasenmäher
fertilizer	Dünger
seeds	Samen Saaten
major	hier: gross
tiles	Fliesen, Kacheln
maintenance	Wartung

For the irregular verbs in this story which are all in the past tense please refer to the "ABC of irregular verbs" in the annex of this book.

Comprehension exercise

Please answer the following questions in full sentences.

1 Why was Michael given compensation?
2 What were his plans for the coming weekend?
3 How was the problem with accommodation solved?
4 Where did they meet?
5 What did they get to eat and drink that evening?
6 What is Gordon's job?
7 How did Gerry know they were in this particular pub?
8 Why are D.I.Y. stores so popular these days?
9 Why do the British have so many gardens?
10 Which basic tools do they need for gardening?

Section 2 Basics

2.1 The structures of the management of a company

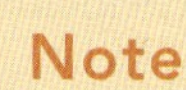

Note

The terminology contained in this worksheet is a guideline only. The meanings and the application of these words may slightly differ from company to company.

the company/the firm	=	die Firma/das Unternehmen
to abbreviate	=	abkürzen (Wörter)
the abbreviation	=	die Abkürzung
a limited liability company = Ltd	=	brit. Gesellschaftsform, entspricht der GmbH
a public limited company = plc	=	brit. Gesellschaftsform, entspricht der AG
to share	=	teilen
the shares	=	die Gesellschaftsanteile, die Aktien
the shareholders	=	die Anteilseigner, die Aktionäre
dividend	=	Dividende, Gewinnbeteiligung
to direct	=	anweisen, anleiten, die Richtung vorgeben
the director	=	nach britischem Recht der Firmeneigner/die Firmeneigner; wer die Anteile besitzt, ist befugt, in seiner Firma Anweisungen zu geben

the board of directors	=	der Vorstand
a member of the board	=	Vorstandsmitglied
the chairman of the board/ president	=	Vorstandsvorsitzender
to chair a meeting	=	eine Sitzung leiten
to decide	=	entscheiden, beschließen
the decision	=	Entscheidung, Beschluß
to make decisions	=	Entscheidungen fällen
boardroom	=	Sitzungszimmer des Vorstands
board secretary	=	Vorstandssekretär/in
board meeting	=	Vorstandssitzung
the minutes of a meeting	=	Sitzungsprotokoll
to keep the minutes of the meeting	=	das Sitzungsprotokoll führen
the office	=	hier: das Amt, das jemand bekleidet
officer	=	Amtsinhaber, auch: leitender Angestellter
the stipulations of the tariff	=	die Bestimmungen des Tarifs
to be applicable for s.o.	=	auf jemanden anwendbar sein
to hold an office	=	ein Amt bekleiden
official	=	offiziell
to execute	=	ausführen
the execution	=	die Ausführung
CEO = chief executive officer	=	der Geschäftsführer (normalerweise ein leitender Angestellter, der die Anweisungen des Vorstands ausführen muss)
CFO = chief financial officer	=	Finanzchef, kaufmännischer Leiter
CPO = chief personnel officer	=	Personalchef
CSO = chief staff officer	=	Personalchef (für die Belegschaft einer Firma sind zwei Begriffe gängig, nämlich „staff" und „personnel")
CTO = chief technical officer	=	technischer Leiter (z.B. in einer Maschinenbaufirma)

to manage	=	leiten
the manager	=	Leiter
the assistant manager	=	der stellvertretende Leiter
the managing director	=	geschäftsführendes Vorstandsmitglied
president & CEO	=	alternative Bezeichnung für das geschäftsführende Vorstandsmitglied
the AGM = annual general meeting	=	die gesetzlich vorgeschriebene Jahreshauptversammlung einer Kapitalgesellschaft
the agenda	=	die Tagesordnung
to supervise	=	überwachen, beaufsichtigen
supervision	=	die Aufsicht
the supervisory board	=	der Aufsichtsrat/Verwaltungsrat
chairman of the supervisory board	=	der Aufsichtsratsvorsitzende
to employ	=	beschäftigen
employment	=	das Beschäftigungsverhältnis
the employer	=	der Arbeitgeber
the employee	=	der Arbeitnehmer
trade union	=	die Gewerkschaft
shop steward	=	der Gewerkschaftssekretär
to negotiate	=	verhandeln
the negotiation	=	die Verhandlung
to enter negotiations	=	die Verhandlungen aufnehmen
to be unemployed	=	arbeitslos sein
labour office	=	Arbeitsamt

2.2 A job application

advertising	=	Werbung
to advertise	=	annoncieren
the job advertisement/advert/ad	=	Stellenanzeige

the position	=	die Stellung
vacant	=	frei
vacancy	=	freie Stelle
the company has a vacancy for a	=	die Fa. hat eine freie Stelle für ....
to man a position	=	eine Stelle besetzen
personnel/staff	=	Belegschaft/Personal
to apply for a job	=	sich bewerben
the application	=	Bewerbung
a successful application	=	die erfolgreiche Bewerbung
the applicant	=	der Bewerber/die Bewerberin
the remuneration	=	die Vergütung
salary	=	Gehalt
wages	=	Wochenlohn
fringe benefits	=	außertarifliche Vergünstigungen (z.B. Firmenwagen, billiger Einkauf)
letter of application	=	die schriftliche Bewerbung
to produce	=	vorlegen, vorzeigen
CV = curriculum vitae	=	Lebenslauf
school reports	=	Schulzeugnisse
references	=	Arbeitszeugnisse, Referenzen
qualifications	=	Qualifikationen
the shortlist	=	die engere Wahl
The applicant was put on the shortlist.	=	der Bewerber wurde in die engere Wahl gezogen
to invite	=	einladen
the invitation	=	die Einladung
to interview	=	befragen
the job interview	=	das Vorstellungsgespräch
to accept an applicant	=	einen Bewerber annehmen
to reject an applicant	=	einen Bewerber ablehnen

the contract	=	der Arbeitsvertrag
to sign	=	unterschreiben
the signature	=	die Unterschrift
health insurance	=	Krankenkasse

2.3 Shops in town

The department store

The typical department store is usually bigger than a supermarket, and the range of products is different. In the supermarket the main emphasis is on food. In a department store, on the other hand, there usually is also a food department (often called the "food hall"), but there are many other departments which a supermarket does not have. Let us have a look at the departments of a typical department store:

store directory	=	Anzeigetafel/Wegweiser
A		
antiques	=	Antiquitäten
audivisual equipment	=	Audio- und Videobedarf, TV, DVD
B		
baby wear	=	Babyausstattung
bank	=	Bankzweigstelle
bathroom articles	=	Badezimmerausstattung
beauty/cosmetics	=	Schönheitspflege
beds, mattresses & bedding	=	Betten und Bettwäsche
books	=	Bücher
C		
carpets	=	Teppiche
children's clothing	=	Kinderbekleidung
children's shoes	=	Kinderschuhe
china	=	Porzellan
computer hardware and software	=	Computer und Zubehör
confectionery	=	Süßwaren

D		
decorative accessories	=	Dekorationsartikel
delivery service	=	Lieferdienst
dinnerware, glassware and silverware	=	Geschirr- und Silberwaren
E		
electrical goods & tools	=	Elektrogeräte und -werkzeuge
F		
fitting rooms	=	Anprobekabinen
food hall	=	Lebensmittelabteilung
G		
gifts	=	Geschenke
H		
haberdashery	=	Kurzwaren
home furnishings	=	Möbel
household appliances	=	Haushaltsgeräte
I		
information	=	Information
K		
kitchenware	=	Küchenausstattung
L		
leather goods	=	Lederwaren
lighting	=	Lampen
lingerie	=	Damenwäsche
linen	=	Haushaltswäsche
luggage	=	Koffer & Reisetaschen
M		
main cash office	=	Hauptkasse
men's shoes	=	Herrenschuhe
men's wear	=	Herren-Oberbekleidung

Mr Minute	=	Schuhreparatur- und Schlüsseldienst
music	=	Musik
N		
newsagent	=	Zeitungen und Zeitschriften
P		
perfumery	=	Parfümerie
S		
shirts & ties	=	Hemden und Krawatten
sports	=	Sportartikel
stationery	=	Schreibwaren
T		
tobacconist	=	Tabakwaren
toilets	=	Toiletten
toys	=	Spielwaren
travel agency	=	Reisebüro
W		
watches and jewellery	=	Uhren und Schmuck
women's wear	=	Damen-Oberbekleidung
women's shoes	=	Damenschuhe

Other shops in town – the retail

the corner shop	=	der "Tante Emma-Laden"
A		
art shop	=	Kunsthandlung
B		
bakery	=	die Bäckerei
bank	=	Bank
barber's shop	=	Herrenfriseur
book shop	=	Buchhandel
boutique	=	Boutique

building society	=	Bausparkasse
butchery	=	die Schlachterei/Metzgerei
C		
camera shop	=	Fotogeschäft
chemistry	=	Drogerie
computer shop	=	Computergeschäft
confectioner	=	Konditor/Süßwarengeschäft
D		
dairy shop	=	Milchgeschäft
E		
estate agent	=	Immobilienmakler
F		
fishmonger	=	der Fischhändler
florist	=	Blumengeschäft
furniture shop	=	Möbelgeschäft
G		
gent's tailor	=	Herrenschneider
greengrocer's	=	Obst- und Gemüsehändler
grocery	=	Lebensmittelgeschäft
H		
haberdashery	=	Kurzwarengeschäft
I		
insurance broker	=	Versicherungsmakler
insurance agent	=	Versicherungsvertreter
ironmonger	=	Eisenwarengeschäft
L		
ladies' hairdresser	=	Damenfriseur
ladies' tailor	=	Damenschneider
laundry	=	Reinigung
lawyer	=	Rechtsanwalt

N		
newsagent	=	Zeitungshändler
O		
off licence	=	Wein- und Spirituosengeschäft
P		
pawnbroker	=	Pfandleihe
pet shop	=	Tierhandlung
pharmacy	=	Apotheke
R		
record shop	=	Musikgeschäft
restaurant	=	Restaurant
S		
savings bank	=	Sparkasse (in GB nicht mehr bekannt)
shoe shop	=	Schuhgeschäft
snack bar	=	Schnellimbiss
T		
tobacconist	=	Tabakwarenladen
toy shop	=	Spielwarengeschäft
travel agency	=	Reisebüro

Section 3 Brush up your grammar

3.1 "W"-questions *Fragestellung mit „W"-Wörtern*

Bisher haben wir über Fragen gesprochen, die man mit „ja“ und „nein“ beantworten kann. Manchmal benötigen wir aber eine genauere Antwort. In diesen Fällen bilden wir Fragen mit einem Fragewort. Wir nennen sie "w-words" da sie fast alle mit einem „w“ beginnen. Nur "how" endet mit einem "w".

Beispiele:

Where did you come from? — I came from school.
Why did you call him? — I called him because I needed his help.
How did you like the meal? — I liked it a lot. It tasted fantastic.

Die am häufigsten verwendeten „W"-Wörter sind:

w-word	Das benutzen wir zum Fragen nach	Beispiele
when	the time	When did he arrive? He arrived at 6 o'clock.
where	the place	Where did you buy this? I bought it at the supermarket.
which	a special person or thing	Which person did he talk to? He talked to the manager. Which lesson do you like best? I like the English lesson best. In questions with "which" we must add a noun after the w-word like in the examples above.
why	a reason	Why did they stop? They stopped because a tyre was flat.
whose	a relationship or a possession	Whose car did you borrow? We borrowed Mr Brown's car. Whose mother did you meet at TESCO? I met Dinah's mother there. In questions with "whose" we also add a noun or a name like in the examples.
who*)	a person	Who did you see at the party? I saw Mr Swan at the party.
what	a thing	What did David find in the newspaper? He found a job advert.
how	a way to do something or how something is	How did you get so wet? I got wet from the rain.

Wie man an den obigen Beispielen sehen kann, muss auch in W-Fragen eine Form von "to do" benutzt werden. Die Form von "to do" zeigt die Zeitform an (do/does = Gegenwart/did = Vergangenheit. Ausnahmen sind Sätze mit Hilfsverben und "to be".

EXERCISE:

Please ask for the underlined part of the sentences. Use the correct question word.

1 Michael saw a job advertisement in the newspaper two months ago.
2 It offered two jobs in Aldershot.
3 Peter applied for the job of a shop assistant.
4 He went to Aldershot by train two weeks later.
5 He wanted to be on time, because he had a job interview.
6 He borrowed his brother's good suit for the interview.
7 He met another applicant at the enterprise.
8 The young man had an interview at 4 pm.

3.2 The "if"-clauses *Der Bedingungssatz/Konditionalsatz*

Es gibt zwar eine ganze Reihe von Bedingungssätzen, die wir aber nicht alle unbedingt brauchen. Wichtig beim Umgang mit Kunden sind die Bedingungssätze I und II.

Merksatz für Bedingungssatz I:

If I give you ..... will you...

z.B.: If I give you the money for it, will you buy a car?
Wenn ich Dir das Geld dafür gebe, wirst Du Dir ein Auto kaufen?

Wenn im „if"-Satz das Verb in der Gegenwart steht, dann muss in der zweiten Satzhälfte unbedingt das Wort „will" erscheinen.

Merksatz für Bedingungssatz II:

If I gave you ..... would you...

z.B.: If I gave you the money for it, would you buy a car?
Wenn ich Dir das Geld dafür gäbe, würdest Du Dir ein Auto kaufen?

Wenn im "if"-Satz das Verb in der Vergangenheit steht, dann muss in der zweiten Satzhälfte unbedingt das Wort „would" erscheinen.

Bedingungssätze müssen nicht mit "if" beginnen, da man den Satzaufbau auch umstellen kann.

Beispiel BS I: Will you buy a car if I give you the money for it?

Beispiel BS II: Would you buy a car if I gave you the money for it?

"Will" und "would" dürfen nie im if-Satz stehen.

Eselsbrücke: "Would" und "will" macht den "if"-Satz schrill.

3.3 False friends *Falsche Freunde*

Falsche Freunde sind ganz üble Gesellen, die uns sowohl im Leben als auch bei der Fremdsprache das Leben schwer machen. Deswegen müssen wir uns vor ihnen in Acht nehmen. In der englischen Sprache bezeichnen wir als falsche Freunde bestimmte Wörter, die genauso aussehen wie die entsprechenden deutschen Wörter, die aber eine vollkommen andere Bedeutung haben. Deswegen dürfen sie auch auf keinen Fall 1:1 übersetzt werden, denn sonst wird der übersetzte Text fehlerhaft oder im schlimmsten Fall sogar sinnlos. Hier ist jetzt eine Aufstellung der wichtigsten falschen Freunde, aber natürlich ist diese Ausstellung nicht vollständig, denn es gibt noch viele andere solche Wörter.

englisches Wort	das heißt auf keinen Fall	sondern
alley	Allee	dunkle Gasse
also	also	auch
ample	Ampel	reichlich
bank	Sitzbank	Kreditinstitut, Flussufer
barracks	Baracke	Kaserne
become (to)	bekommen	werden
billion	eine Billion	Milliarde
chef	Chef	Koch
construct (to)	konstruieren	bauen
control (to)	kontrollieren	steuern, lenken, regeln
corn	Getreide	Mais
creep (to)	kriechen	schleichen
eventually	eventuell	schließlich, endlich
fabric	Fabrik	Stoff, Gewebe
gift	Gift	Geschenk
mist	Mist	Frühnebel
neck	Nacken	Hals
physician	Physiker	prakt. Arzt
pudding	Pudding	Speise, die Mehl enthält (black pudding, Christmas pudding)
speck	Speck	Schmutzfleck
spend (to)	spenden	Zeit verbringen Geld ausgeben
town hall	Stadthalle	Rathaus
warehouse	Warenhaus, Kaufhaus	Lagerhalle
wonder (to)	sich wundern	sich fragen

Section 4 Practise your word power

4.1 Exercise Word groups

Put each of the words below into the correct list. *Use each word only once!*
Can you think of more words to add to each list?

milk syrup corned beef honey flour beer shoe polish
margarine sugar wine peanut butter fruits cream jam salt
vinegar toothpaste oil cashew nuts yoghurt mustard
oatmeal mineral water mustard sour cream spices tomato puree
cooking fat rice marmalade tartar sauce mayonnaise mayonnaise
Coke baked beans herring in tomato sauce

1 Sold in bags

....
....
....
....
....
....

2 Sold in jars

....
....
....
....
....
....

3 Sold in bottles

....
....
....
....
....
....

4 Sold in tins

....
....
....
....
....
....

5 Sold in tubes

....
....
....
....
....
....

6 Sold in cups

....
....
....
....
....
....

4.2 Exercise Odd man out

Only one answer is right. Which one is it?

1 One of these is not a drink. Which one is it?
a corn b rum c whisky
d brandy e gin

2 Your father's grandfather is your
a grandfather b uncle c great grandfather
d forefather e stepfather

3 One of these is sticky. Which one is it?
a water b wine c honey
d rice e cornfalkes

4 A salmon is a
a mammal b insect c bird
d rodent e fish

5 One of these is not a mammal. Which one is it? (a mammal is an animal that feeds its babies with milk)
a cow b sow c partridge
d lamb e goat

6 One of these is not a vegetable. Which one is it?
a leek b curly kail c blackcurrant
d egg plant e black salsify

7 One of these is not made from milk. Which one is it?
a cream b cheese c butter
d buttermilk e buttercup

8 The colour of a daffodil is
a blue b white c black
d yellow e green

9 One of these has nothing to do with electricity. Which one is it?
a AC b DC c socket
d plug e stream

10 The favourite snack of the Germans is
a raw fish and rice b fish & chips c fish & crisps
d barbequed sausage + curry powder e sour kidneys

11 One of these does not grow in Germany. Which one is it?
a peanut b garlic c sweet green pepper
d asparagus e hazelnut

12 One of these words in the plural is wrong. Which one?
a heroes b photoes c tomatoes
d potatoes e zeroes

13 Which of these can be poisonous? *(poisonous = giftig)*
a cucumber b avocado c potato
d almond e mushroom

14 Mustard is sold in jars. Which other container is also used?
a bottle b bag c jug
d sack e tube

15 A slice of beef which we fry in the frying pan is a
a steak b chip c slab
d piece e chalk

16 Where would you have to go if you wanted to buy nails and screws?
a barber b florist c ironmonger
d butcher e grocer

17 One of these has no feathers. Which one is it?
a turkey b partridge c guinea fowl
d snail e eagle

18 The informal way of saying "to eat" is
a to have a nosh b to fall asleep c to knock off
d to idle e to booze

19 One of these is different from the others - it has no legs. Which one is it?
a goat b snake c rat
d guinea pig e stork

20 The most exclusive department store in the world is
a Woolworth b Marks & Spencer c Harrods
d Littlewoods e Tesco

4.3 Exercise Definitions

barber CFO saucer CV feathers florist wool pound bus leather chairman of the board CPO spoon scales wages Boxing Day brother shelf petrol salary

1 The big boss of a company is the
2 The money you get for your work is your
3 The boss of the personnel is the
4 The person responsible for the money in a company is the
5 The written story of your life is the
6 100 pence are a
7 where men get a haircut
8 Workers and craftsmen earn
9 a device we use for weighing food
10 Pullovers and cardigans are made of
11 a big motor vehicle with many seats for passengers
12 cup and
13 the device we eat soup with
14 a device in a shop for keeping things on
15 the material shoes are usually made of
16 the "dress" birds wear
17 Your father's other son is your
18 without it, your car would not move
19 A shop where you can buy roses is a
20 The 26th of December is

4.4 Exercise Fill the gaps

Oxford Street – shopper's paradise in central London

As mentioned before, Michael was very interested in Gordon's work. So after their .... *(Mahlzeit)* he again listened carefully to what Gordon told him, and he only .... *(unterbrechen)* him every now and then to ask some additional questions. Gordon told him everything about his job in the very big and exclusive department store in Oxford Street where he works in the men's sportswear department and sells .... *(Tennisschläger)*. This is the ideal job for him because he is a keen sportsman, his favourite sport, of course, is tennis. Clearwoods & Sons in Oxford Street is in a very big building with seven .... *(Stockwerke)*, and there are some 50 departments and sub-departments in it. Now Gordon tried to .... *(erklären)* to Michael how many departments there are exactly in the store in Oxford Street, but he could not manage, there are simply too many. There are of course the usual ones such as a large food hall in the .... *(Untergeschoss)* and large departments for household appliances (e.g. freezers, ... *[Kühlschränke]*, washing machines and .... *[Wäschetrockner]*), audivisual equipment (TVs, radios, DVD-players etc.), a large computer department, but also a very exclusive .... *(Geschenke)* department, a perfume department (very exclusive and expensive), an even more exclusive department for watches and .... *(Schmuck)*, a department for dinnerware, glassware and silverware (also quite exclusive) and, of course, a large .... *(Spielzeug)* department. Michael wanted to know how many different items they usually had in stock, but Gordon did not know, he simply said "Sorry, mate, it is an awful lot, that's all I know. But I tell you what – come and look yourself. You will still be here on Monday, just come in and see me in my department. I am sure I will be given the time to show you around for an hour or so." Michael did not .... *(zögern)* to promise that he would come.

Later on that evening, Gordon's friend Gerry turned up and joined the two Gordon had sent him an SMS that they would be in "The Sherlock" all evening. Gerry .... *(wohnen)* in Lambeth on the other side of the River Thames, and he worked in a big D.I.Y. superstore in Hammersmith.

Now Michael could also learn a few things about a D.I.Y. store and what the work in such a store is like. He eagerly began to ask questions, and Gerry .... *(geduldig)* tried to answer them all. Most .... *(Briten)* have a house, and nearly every house in the U.K. has a garden. That is why gardening is the hobby of millions of people in the U.K., and for this hobby they require a large number of tools (.................... *[Spaten]*, hoe, rake, ... *[Rasenmäher]*), plants and other things. The idea of D.I.Y. stores is not that old. The first ones appeared some 20 years ago, but now they are extremely .... *(beliebt)*, not only in the U.K. Besides gardening, more and more people do most of the repairs in their houses and .... *(Wohnungen)* themselves, and quite a few even do major jobs such as rebuilding a .... *(Badezimmer)* which requires a lot of special tools and other equipment. The store Gerry works in is one of the biggest in London, and so Gerry explained to Michael the range of products such a store usually stocks: basic building materials (bricks, cement) including covering materials and insulating materials, ... *(Fliesen)*, lamps, ... *(Glühbirnen)*, cables and fuses, wood and wood-based materials, all sorts of tools and power tools, paints and .... *(Tapeten)*, bathroom installations, ... *(alles)* you need for gardening including tools and plants, special clothing, tools and materials for car maintenance and repair, tools and materials for bicycle maintenance and repair, to mention only a few. Gerry told Michael that they stock approx. 100.000 different items in his store. Michael was deeply .... *(beeindruckt)* – four times as much as in his own supermarket.

Unit 7

Section 1 Texts

Text 1 Life is full of surprises

All in all, Michael Crocker was quite happy with his situation. His job was all right, even though the training methods in Britain differ very much from the ones he knew from Germany. His mother was very happy with her job in London, his sisters were at home again. They had left the boarding school at the end of the last term. And his father now was
5 usually at home in the evening because he had an office job. There were no more exercises he had to go on. But every now and then Michael felt a little bit homesick. Life is different in England, and he had spent a large part of his life in Germany. He began to miss some of his friends (even though they regularly had contact by e-mail) and he also missed his grand-parents very much. Sometimes he even missed German food even though his supermarket
10 stocked many specialities from Germany such as "Wurst" which otherwise is not really well-known in Britain. But his grandmother's cooking …
Michael was supervising the stacking of shelves with tinned food when one of his work-mates turned up and told him that the store manager wanted to see him immediately. His workmate had a silly smile on his face. Quite obviously he was thinking that Michael had
15 done something wrong and the manager was going to tell him off. So Michael handed over his job to his workmate who continued to put tins on the shelves together with two other members of the staff. Michael went to the manager's office, knocked on the door and waited for Mr Wellwood to call him in. He was relieved when he saw the smile on the face of Mr Wellwood, so obviously he was not in trouble. "Sit down, Michael" said Mr. Wellwood.
20 "I have called you to discuss a few things with you. It is about your prospects, your future career. You have done a very good job in our market so far, but I don't think you would like to stack shelves forever. There are better things you could do with the experiences and the language skills you have!" "Oh yes, Mr Wellwood" replied Michael, "I am glad you mentioned my future in the company

25 I really like to work here, but I also think it is time for me to learn something new and to take over some more responsibility. This in-house course on marketing I went to last month was very interesting, and I would like to learn more about that particular subject. Maybe that will be my future." Mr Wellwood smiled again. "Well, Michael, here is a fax I got from headquarters this morning. They have big plans in London. You know that we have branch-
30 es in many parts of Europe such as France and Belgium and even the Czech Republic, but now they wish to expand their operations to Germany as well. There will be a pilot project, a new supermarket in a town called Neuenhagen in Northern Germany, and I think that this town is not too far away from the place where you used to live. The good news for you is that headquarters are looking for German-speaking members of their team, and we would like
35 you to join this team. What do you think about it?" Michael did not know what to say, he was completely taken by surprise.
But Mr Wellwood carried on: "You have already been earmarked as the assistant of the store manager in the new German supermarket, and you will be responsible for the recruitment of the staff together with the manager. This means that you will require some extra training
40 in the London headquarters of the company before you can go. I have already told Sharon to reserve a place for you on the next course which is due to begin on the first of next month. The course will last six weeks, and during that time you will live in the company guesthouse in central London."
Once again, Michael did not know what to say. He didn't hesitate long, he accepted straight
45 away. That evening, Michael was so excited. He lay in his bed and couldn't sleep a wink all night.

Vocabulary List

differ (to, r)	unterscheiden
feel homesick(to)	Heimweh haben
tell s.o. off (to)	jmd. "zusammenstauchen"
He was ever so excited.	Er war überaus aufgeregt.
He could not sleep a wink.	Er bekam kein Auge zu.

For the irregular verbs in this story which are all in the past tense please refer to the "ABC of irregular verbs" in the annex of this book.

Comprehension exercise

1. Why was Michael quiet happy with his situation?
2. What exactly did he miss when he thought of Germany?
3. Why did the store manager want to see Michael?
4. What were TESCO's plans in respect to Germany?
5. What would Michael have to/take part in before he could go back to Germany?
6. How is the part of the North Sea between the UK and Belgium/France called?
7. What is the difference between driving a car in the U.K. and in Germany?
8. Where did Michael first meet Ian?
9. What was Ian doing to improve his German?
10. Ian had certain difficulties in Germany. What exactly was is?

Text 2 Into a new phase of life

Now Michael sat on the train from Ostend in Belgium to Cologne. He had had a very pleasant crossing from Dover to Ostend, the sea in the Channel was calm and the sun was shining. So he had spent the 75 minutes of the crossing on deck of the ferry. Michael had left his car back in England. His car was fairly old, and of course, it was right-hand drive because in the U.K. you have to drive on the left side of the road. For his new job in Germany, he would have a company car with left-hand drive. In a few days, a new chapter of his life would begin. He leant back in his seat and recalled the events of the past three or four months. First of all, he had successfully finished his marketing course in London, but immediately afterwards he had to go on a follow-on course. This time it was personnel management. He had to learn a lot about recruitment of staff, how to read CVs, how to conduct job interviews and how to conclude contracts of employment. The manager of the new supermarket, whose name was Ian McIntyre, was already in Germany even though the supermarket building was still under construction and their offices were not ready yet. They would have to work in a provisional office in a nearby hotel for some weeks. Michael arrived in Cologne in the late afternoon. The conductor had already told him at which platform his train to Hanover would leave. Michael took his trolley, extended the handle and, with his holdall in the other hand, began to walk over to platform no. 7 where the train to Hanover would leave in approx. 20 minutes time. Suddenly his mobile phone began to buzz. He looked at the display. It was an SMS from Ian. In his message, he asked him what time he would arrive in Hanover and where to pick him up. Ian and Michael had both attended the preparation course at the company headquarters in London, and even though Ian was a few years older than Michael they soon became good friends. Michael now sent an SMS as a reply to Ian in which he told him the arrival time of his train and the platform it would arrive.
Shortly after seven o'clock in the evening his ICE train arrived at Hanover main station, and indeed Ian already waited for him on the platform. They greeted each other with a handshake, and then they took the escalators to the ground floor and walked over to the car park behind the station to Ian's car – a brand-new BMW. Ian unlocked the boot so that Michael could put his luggage in, and then they set off for Neuenhagen.
While he was driving the car through the city of Hanover towards the north-westbound expressway, Ian told Michael about the piles of applications that were already waiting for him. A week ago, he had put a job advertisement into two of the local newspapers, and the response was overwhelming. He also told Michael about the German classes he attended at the local adult education centre, and he said that he managed to improve his German a lot. Ian was very ambitious, and whatever he did - he did it right. Only driving on the right-hand side of the road was still a little bit difficult for him, he had to concentrate himself quite a lot. Michael, of course, had none of these problems, his German was perfect and he was used to the German traffic. He leant back, relaxed and thought of the challenge he was now facing.

Vocabulary List

the Channel	der Ärmelkanal
a chapter of one's life	ein Lebensabschnitt
conductor	hier: Schaffner
holdall	Reisetasche
boot	hier: Kofferraum
provisional	provisorisch, vorläufig
adult education centre	Volkshochschule

For the irregular verbs in this story which are all in the past tense please refer to the "ABC of irregular verbs" in the annex of this book.

Section 2 Basics

2.1 Communications – the telephone (basic vocabulary)

the set (the telephone with all its parts)	der Apparat
to receive	empfangen
the receiver	der Telefonhörer
to dial, dialled, have dialled	wählen
the dial	die Wähleinrichtung am Telefon (Tastatur)
to telephone/to phone	telefonieren
to make a phone call	anrufen
the ring	hier: das Klingeln
to give someone a ring	jemanden anrufen
the number/the phone number	die Telefonnummer
the prefix	die Ortsvorwahl
the code/the country code	die Ländervorwahl
digit	Zahlenstelle
a four-digit number	eine vierstellige Zahl

Example:

0049	5151	1234567
country code	prefix	phone number

Note

The number "0" is pronounced "oh" in telephone numbers

exchange/telephone exchange	=	die Telefonvermittlung (in vielen Anglo-Amerikanischen Ländern wird in Firmen noch per Hand vermittelt.)
operator the person (male or female) who works in a telephone exchange	=	Telefonist/Telefonistin

Note

When you talk to the switchboard operator, you usually address this person as "exchange".

extension/ext. = extension	Anschluss, Apparat
the line	die Verbindung
The line is bad.	Die Verbindung ist schlecht.
to hang up	auflegen, beenden
to close a call	ein Gespräch beenden
busy/engaged	besetzt
The number is engaged. The line is busy.	Auf dem Apparat wird gesprochen.
the engaged tone	das Besetztzeichen
the reply	die Antwort
Hold the line, please.	Bitte bleiben Sie am Apparat.
Mr./Mrs. XYZ is on the phone.	Herr XYZ ist am Apparat.

Note

The most important phrase when you talk to customers is:

I would like to ….

Examples:

I would like to speak to

I would like to have word with ….. *Ich möchte mit … sprechen.*

to speak up	lauter sprechen
to speak slowly	langsam sprechen
I didn't get that.	Das habe ich nicht verstanden.
to repeat	wiederholen
to spell	buchstabieren
the spelling	das Buchstabieren, die Schreibweise
letter	Buchstabe
sentence	Satz
previous	vorher, vorangegangen, das vorherige …
telephone directory/phone book	Telefonbuch
yellow pages	Gelbe Seiten
to look s.th. up	etwas nachschlagen
the message	die Nachricht
to remind s.o. of s.th.	jmd. an etwas erinnern
to take a note of s.th.	eine Notiz von etwas machen
to interrupt	unterbrechen
the interruption	die Unterbrechung
the matter	die Angelegenheit
important	wichtig
urgent	dringend
to apologize	entschuldigen
the apology	die Entschuldigung

Some important country codes:

Germany	*0049*		
Australia	*0061*	*Austria*	*0043*
Belgium	*0032*	*Denmark*	*0045*
France	*0033*	*Italy*	*0039*
Poland	*0048*	*Russia*	*007*

Switzerland	*0041*	*The Netherlands*	*0031*
United Kingdom	*0044*	*United States*	*001*

Some useful phrases on the telephone *Nützliche Redewendungen am Telefon*

The opening of a telephone call:	*Die Eröffnung eines Telefongespräches:*
Good morning, ….	*(wird bis ca. 12.00 Uhr gesagt)*
Good afternoon, ...	*(wird von 12.00 bis ca. 18.00 Uhr gesagt)*
Good evening, ...	*(wird nach 18.00 Uhr gesagt)*

Good morning, exchange, please put me through to extension 1234, please.
Guten Morgen, Vermittlung, bitte stellen Sie mich zu Apparat 1234 durch.

Good morning, exchange, please connect me with/to extension 1234, please.
Guten Morgen, Vermittlung, bitte verbinden Sie mich mit Apparat 1234.

Sorry, I don't know his/her extension. Could you put me through, please?
Es tut mir leid, ich weiß die Nummer nicht. Können Sie mich bitte durchstellen?

I would like to speak to Mr/Mrs/Miss .... personally.
Ich möchte mit Herrn/Frau .... persönlich sprechen.

Hello, this is .... . I would like to speak to …..
Hallo, hier ist ….. Ich möchte gern mit .... sprechen.

This is not a private call, it is an official call.
Das ist kein Privatgespräch, das ist ein dienstliches Gespräch.

I am still waiting to be connected.
Ich warte immer noch darauf, dass ich verbunden werde.

This is a long-distance call. I can't wait any longer.
Das ist ein Ferngespräch. Ich kann nicht länger warten.

Could you try again, please?
Können Sie es bitte noch einmal versuchen?

How can I help you?
Wie kann ich Ihnen helfen?

The reason why I am calling is ….
Der Grund für meinen Anruf ist…..

My extension is 1234.
Meine Durchwahl ist 1234.

I am on extension 1234.
Ich bin auf dem Apparat 1234 zu erreichen.

Am I speaking to Mr/Mrs/Mis ....?
Spreche ich mit Herrn/Frau …?

Could you put me back to the exchange, please?
Können Sie mich bitte zur Vermittlung zurückstellen?

How to leave/take a message: *Wie man eine Nachricht hinterlässt/annimmt:*

I would like to leave a message for ....
Ich möchte für ... eine Nachricht hinterlassen.

Please take a message for Mr ....
Bitte nehmen Sie eine Nachricht für Herrn ... auf.

Can I take a message?
Kann ich etwas ausrichten?

General expressions *Allgemeine Redewendungen*

I am afraid my English is not very good.
Ich fürchte mein Englisch ist nicht sehr gut.

Sorry to interrupt you, but ....
Entschuldigen Sie, dass ich Sie unterbreche, aber ...

I am very short of time.
Ich habe nur sehr wenig Zeit.

I am afraid Mr/Mrs/Miss .... is not available.
Leider ist Herr/Frau .... nicht zu sprechen.

I will see if I can find him/her.
Ich werde sehen, ob ich ihn/sie finden kann.

How to pass general information: *Wie man allgemeine Informationen weitergibt:*

The country code for Germany is 0049 (double-oh four nine)
Die Ländervorwahl für Deutschland ist 0049.

The prefix for Cologne is .....
Die Ortsvorwahl für Köln ist ....

Could you give me your name, please?
Könnten Sie mir bitte Ihren Namen sagen?

I would like to have some information about ...
Ich möchte bitte einige Informationen über ... haben.

What company are you from?
Von welcher Firma sind Sie?

Would you please leave me your name/phone number/address?
Bitte hinterlassen Sie mir Ihren Namen/Telefonnummer/Adresse.

Would you mind telling me what you are calling about?
Würden Sie mir bitte den Grund Ihres Anrufs nennen?

Can Mr/Mrs/Miss .... be reached by mobile phone?
Kann ich Herrn/Frau .... über Handy erreichen?

I can also be reached by mobile phone. My number is….
Ich kann auch über Handy erreicht werden. Meine Nummer ist ....

Sorry I kept you waiting.
Entschuldigen Sie, dass ich Sie habe warten lassen.

Sorry, you have dialled the wrong number.
Es tut mir leid, Sie haben falsch gewählt.

Sorry to have troubled you.
Entschuldigen Sie die Störung.

When the line is bad: *Wenn die Verbindung schlecht ist:*

Could you speak up, please.
Können Sie bitte lauter sprechen.

Could you speak slowly, please.
Können Sie bitte langsamer sprechen.

Please repeat.
Bitte wiederholen.

Please repeat the last word.
Bitte wiederholen Sie das letzte Wort.

Please repeat the last sentence.
Bitte wiederholen Sie den letzten Satz.

Please repeat everything before …….
Bitte wiederholen Sie alles vor ....

Please repeat everything after …...
Bitte wiederholen Sie alles nach ......

Could you spell it, please?
Können Sie das bitte buchstabieren?

I will spell the word: ….
Ich werde das Wort buchstabieren: ...

Have you got that?
Haben Sie das?

I can hardly hear your.
Ich kann Sie kaum verstehen.

We have got a crossed line.
Da ist noch jemand in der Leitung.

How to ask for a return call: *Wie man um einen Rückruf bittet:*

Could you ask Mr/Mrs/Miss …to call me back, please?
Können Sie Herrn/Frau … bitten, mich zurückzurufen?

Mr/Mrs/Miss … asked me to call you back.
Herr/Frau … bat mich, Sie zurückzurufen.

I am returning your call.
Ich sollte Sie zurückrufen.

When shall I call you back?
Wann soll ich Sie zurückrufen?

Please try again tomorrow/next Monday etc.
Bitte versuchen Sie es morgen/nächsten Montag etc. noch einmal

Would you please tell him/her that … called?
Würden Sie ihm/ihr bitte ausrichten, dass … angerufen hat?

To conclude/close a call: *Zur Beendigung des Gespräches:*

Anything else I can do for your?
Kann ich noch etwas für Sie tun?

You can phone me/us on 1234567.
Sie können mich/uns unter der Nummer 1234567 erreichen.

Thank you for calling.
Vielen Dank für Ihren Anruf.

It has been nice talking to you.
Es war nett mit Ihnen zu sprechen.

The spelling alphabet

Sometimes the line can be bad and the person at the other end is difficult to understand or you are difficult to understand. In such cases it is best to spell the important words in your message. To do so, you have to use the below words in the spelling alphabet.

A	=	Alpha
B	=	Bravo
C	=	Charlie
D	=	Delta
E	=	Echo
F	=	Foxtrott
G	=	Golf
H	=	Hotel
I	=	India
J	=	Julliett
K	=	Kilo
L	=	Lima
M	=	Mike

N	=	November
O	=	Oscar
P	=	Papa
Q	=	Quebec
R	=	Romeo
S	=	Sierra
T	=	Tango
U	=	Uniform
V	=	Victor
W	=	Whisky
X	=	X-ray
Y	=	Yankee
Z	=	Zulu

2.2 Commonly used abbreviations

Häufig verwendete Abkürzungen

To "abbreviate" means to make a long word short. In the English language we have quite a large number of abbreviations, many of these are used in e-mails and SMS. Here are some of the most commonly used ones:

abbreviation	to be pronounced as	German meaning
AC	alternating current	Wechselstrom
afaik	as far as I know	soweit ich weiß ....
approx.	approximately	ungefähr, cirka
aka	also known as	auch als ... bekannt
asap	as soon as possible	so schnell wie möglich
ATM	automated teller machine	Geldautomat
attn	attention	zur Kenntnisnahme
CEO	chief executive officer	Geschäftsführer
CSO/CPO	chief personnel officer	Personalchef
CFO	chief financial officer	Finanzchef/kaufmännischer Leiter
CTO	chief technical officer	technischer Leiter
cwt	hundredweight	50,4 kg, entspricht unserem Zentner
DC	direct current	Gleichstrom
e.g.	for example	zum Beispiel
FAQ	frequently asked questions	oft gestellte Fragen
ft	foot	Fuß (Längenmass, 30 cm)
FRG	Federal Republic of Germany Bundesrepublik Deutschland	
i.e.	that means	das heißt, das bedeutet
imho	in my humble opinion	meiner bescheidenen Meinung nach
lb	pound	Pfund (Gewicht, 454 g)
oz	ounce	Unnze (ca. 31 g, für Feingold)
rpm	revolutions per minute	Umdrehungen pro Minute
U.K.	United Kingdom of Great Britain and Northern Ireland	Vereinigtes Königreich

abbreviation	to be pronounced as	German meaning
VAT	value-added tax	Mehrwertsteuer
wef	with effect from	mit Wirkung vom ....

Section 3 Brush up your grammar

3.1 Adjective or adverb? *Adjektiv oder Adverb?*

Während Adjektive (Eigenschaftswörter) uns sagen wie etwas ist (sie beschreiben das Nomen im Satz), geben uns Adverbien Informationen wie jemand etwas tut. Da Adverbien im Englischen sehr oft die Endsilbe –ly haben, müssen wir zwischen Adverbien und Adjektiven unterscheiden.

Beispiel: Michael is a careful driver.
He drives carefully.

Sehen Sie sich bitte die folgenden Beispiele an und achten Sie darauf, auf welchen Teil des Satzes sich die **Adjektive** beziehen:

Michael is a careful driver.	In beiden Sätzen erfahren wir etwas über die Qualität des Nomens. Deswegen können wir sagen: **Adjektive beschreiben Nomen.**
Michael is always careful.	

Das nächste Beispiel beschreibt den Gebrauch von Adverbien:

Michael drives carefully.	Hier bekommen wir Information darüber, wie jemand etwas tut . Wir bekommen also Information über das Verb. **Adverbien modifizieren Verben.**
Michael drives extremely carefully.	Dieses Adverb beschreibt, wie vorsichtig Michael etwas tut . **Adverbien beschreiben andere Adverbien.**
Michael is an extremely careful driver.	Hier gibt das Adverb Information über die Qualität des Nomens. **Adverbien beschreiben Adjektive.**
Luckily Michael got his driving licence.	Dieses Adverb gibt Informationen über die Qualität des ganzen Satzes. **Adverbien verändern ganze Sätze.**

Aufgepasst:

Our dog Ben smells badly. (Ben is old. He can not smell very well anymore.)
Our dog Ben smells bad. (Ben needs a bath.)

Adjektive beschreiben Verben der Wahrnehmung. Nur wenn das Verb der Wahrnehmung auf eine Handlung hinweist, benutzen wir Adverbien zur Beschreibung dieser Handlung.

Bildung von Adverbien

Wenn wir in der englischen Sprache Adverbien bilden, dann hängen wir die Endung –ly an das entsprechende Adjektiv:

slow > slowly, general > generally, usual > usually, exact > exactly, complete > completely,

Wenn das Adjektiv mit –le endet, entfällt das -e am Ende:
simple > simply, gentle > gently

Bei Adjektiven mit der Endung –y, verwandelt sich dieses y in ein i. Dann fügen wir das –ly an:
easy > easily, clumsy > clumsily, …

Einige Adjektive enden aber schon mit –ly. Diese Adjekive bilden Adverbien wie:
friendly > in a friendly way, lovely > in a lovely way, silly > in a silly way.

Einige Adjektive und Adverbien sind identisch:
She gets up early. > She is an early bird.
He can run very fast. > He is a fast runner.
They don't play fair. > It is not a fair game.

…

Das Adjektiv good hat als Adverb die Sonderform well.

Exercise

And now it is your turn. Adjective or adverb?
Please put the words in brackets into the correct form.

1 This is an (easy) and (useful) exercise.
2 (Hopeful) you can (easy) fill in the (correct) forms.
3 David had an (exciting) day at the supermarket.
4 While he was listening (careful) to Gwen's explanations, he (sudden) realized that a red light was flashing (irregular) at the bottom of the cheese counter.
5 He thought, this was (nomal) and so he did not ask about this (flashing) light.
6 He did not want to interrupt Gwen's (interesting) explanations.
7 Some minutes later he was watching the store men, who were (busy) unloading (huge) lorries.
8 They were carrying (big) boxes of (fresh) fish to the fish counter in the market.
9 Gwen was talking in a (loud) voice to him, because it was quite (noisy) there.
10 David was just concentrating to understand Gwen's information, when (sudden) her mobile phone rang.
11 Gwen (slow) took the phone out of her pocket and answered it (friendly).

12 In the meantime Mr Wellwood also had realized the (flashing) light at the cheese counter.
13 He knew that something was (wrong) with the cooling and (immediate) he called Gwen.
14 Together they had to find a (quick) solution because some cheese does not smell (good) when it is getting too warm.

3.2 Exercise Opposites *(Gegenteile)*

All the following words on the list are adjectives. Find the appropriate opposites of them. Make a sentence with both words.

Example: The opposite of black is white.

1	night	___________	14	slow	___________
2	long	___________	15	good	___________
3	wet	___________	16	old (Sachen)	___________
4	expensive	___________	17	old (Mensch)	___________
5	warm	___________	18	soft	___________
6	beautiful	___________	19	clean	___________
7	liquid	___________	20	early	___________
8	much	___________	21	rich	___________
9	positive	___________	22	sad	___________
10	sweet	___________	23	stupid	___________
11	light (Gewicht)	___________	24	light (hell)	___________
12	round	___________	25	come	___________
13	sunny	___________	26	yes	___________

Section 4 Practise your word power

4.1 Exercise Word groups

Put each of the words below into the correct list. *Use each word only once!*
Can you think of more words to add to each list?

train fax big building Harrods tram bar crowded printer cafeteria Westminster chocolate bus Tower monitor SMS ferry Oxford Street escalators software letter DJ taxi Piccadilly Circus many storeys mouse telephone underground keyboard e-mail music computer postcard Buckingham Palace dancing food hall large range of products

1 London

....
....
....
....
....
....

2 Department store

....
....
....
....
....
....

3 Public transport

....
....
....
....
....
....

4 Computer system

....
....
....
....
....
....

5 Discotheque

....
....
....
....
....
....

6 Means of communication

....
....
....
....
....
....

4.2 Exercise Odd man out

Only one answer is right. Which one is it?

1 Eat is to stop being hungry as drink is to stop being
a hot | b thirsty | c wet
d tired | e cold

2 One of these countries has two official national languages. Which one?
a Canada | b Australia | c United States
d Great Britain | e Greece

3 What is the opposite of loud?
a low | b calm | c silent
d noisy | e soft

4 Complete the phrase: dustpan and
a duster | b sponge | c mop
d broom | e brush

5 Which is different?
a coffee | b bear | c beer
d cocoa | e tea

6 All these are public holidays in Germany. One of them is in springtime. Which one is it?
a New Year | b Reunification Day | c Labour Day
d Boxing Day | e New Year's Eve

7 One of these is not edible. Which one is it?
a steak | b pork | c noodles
d china | e cream

8 One of these has nothing to do with playing football.
a pitch | b referee | c racket
d goal | e players

9 Which of these is not a season of the year?
a month | b spring | c autumn
d summer | e winter

10 How often is a salary usually paid?
a once a week | b once a month | c after a job
d twice a month | e every fortnight

11 Which do we not say?
a a pile of tins
b a pile of houses
c a pile of newspapers
d a pile of boxes
e a pile of rubbish

12 The opposite of dangerous is
a safe
b easy
c pleasant
d beautiful
e comfortable

13 Which of these containers will easily hold ten litres?
a bucket
b cup
c tin
d jar
e jug

14 Girl is to woman as girls are to
a womin
b women
c woman's
d wommen
e womans

15 All these are part of your body. Which one will you also find on a clock or watch?
a toe
b foot
c finger
d hand
e leg

16 The opposite of early is
a soon
b slow
c late
d first
e last

17 One of these colours is not on the Union Jack (the British flag). Which one is it?
a white
b red
c blue
d green

18 A room inside the roof of a house is called
a basement
b lobby
c workshop
d storeroom
e attic

19 What is the opposite of "to teach"?
a to show
b to learn
c to know
d to listen
e to understand

20 One of these words is not English. Which one is it?
a gateau
b kindergarten
c to abseil
d brathering
e gathering

4.3 Exercise Definitions

cook glasses coin sour milkman laundry import laptop tea clock sponge staff paper postman counter lamp New Year's Eve Russia stamp veal

1 You soak it with water, and when it is wet enough you clean the blackboard with it.
2 a hot drink the British like very much. They always drink it with milk and sugar.
3 It has a dial and two hands and shows the time.
4 It is above your head and gives light when it is dark.
5 He delivers parcels, postcards and letters.
6 He works in a kitchen and prepares meals
7 He sells butter, cream and cheese.
8 Without them, some people could not see properly.
9 It is thin, made of wood, usually white and we write on it.
10 It is made of metal, round and you pay with it. 11 the place where they clean dirty clothes
12 lemons and vinegar are
13 a small computer you can put on your knees
14 a colourful piece of paper you stick on a letter
15 a big solid table in a bank or shop
16 Another word for personnel is
17 The biggest country in the world is
18 Bringing goods from another country to Germany is
19 Meat from a very young cow is
20 The English meaning of "Silvester" is

4.4 Exercise Fill the gaps

Life is full of .... (Überraschungen)

All in all, Michael Crocker was quite happy with his situation. His job was all right, even though the training methods in Britain .... *(unterscheiden)* very much from the ones he knew from Germany. His mother was very happy with her job in London, his sisters were at home again. They had left the boarding school at the end of the last term. And his father now was usually at home in the evening .... *(weil)* he had an office job, there were no more exercises he had to go on. But every now and then Michael felt a little bit homesick. Life is different in England, and he had spent a large part of his life in Germany. He began to miss some of his friends (even though they regularly had contact by e-mail) and he also missed his grandparents very much. .... *(manchmal)* he even missed German food even though his supermarket stocked many specialities from

Germany such as "Wurst" which otherwise is not really well-known in Britain. But his grandmother's cooking ...
Michael was supervising the stacking of shelves with .... (Lebensmittelkonserven) food when one of his workmates turned up and told him that the store manager wanted to see him .... (unmittelbar, sofort). His workmate had a silly smile on his face. Quite .... (offensichtlich) he was thinking that Michael had done something wrong and the manager was going to tell him off. So Michael handed over his job to his workmate who continued to put tins on the shelves together with two other members of the staff. Michael went to the manager's office, ... (klopfen) on the door and waited for Mr Wellwood to call him in. He was relieved when he saw the smile on the face of Mr Wellwood, so .... (offensichtlich) he was not in trouble. "Sit down, Michael" said Mr. Wellwood. "I have called you to discuss a few things with you. It is about your prospects, your future career. You have done a very good job in our market so far, but I don't think you would like to stack shelves forever. There are better things you could do with the .... (Erfahrungen) and the language skills you have!" "Oh yes, Mr Wellwood" replied Michael, "I am glad you mentioned my future in the company. I really like to work here, but I also think it is time for me to learn .... (etwas) new and to take over some more .... (Verantwortung). This in-house .... (Kurs, Lehrgang) on marketing I went to last month was very interesting, and I would like to learn more about that particular subject. Maybe that will be my future." Mr Wellwood smiled again. "Well, Michael, here is a fax I got from .... (Firmenzentrale) this morning. They have big plans in London. You know that we have branches in many parts of Europe such as France and Belgium and .... (sogar) the Czech Republic, but now they wish to .... (ausdehnen) their operations to Germany as well. There will be a pilot project, a new supermarket in a town called Neuenhagen in Northern Germany, and I think that this town is not too far away from the place where you used to live. The good news for you is that .... (Firmenzentrale) are looking for German-speaking members of their team, and we would like you to join this team. What do you think about it?" – Michael did not know what to say, he was completely taken by .... (Überraschung).
But Mr Wellwood carried on: "You have already been earmarked as the assistant of the store manager in the new German supermarket, and you will be responsible for the

recruitment of the staff .... (*zusammen*) with the manager. This means that you will require some extra training in the London headquarters of the company before you can go. I have .... (*schon*) told Sharon to reserve a place for you on the next .... (*Kurs, Lehrgang*) which is due to begin on the first of next month. The .... (*Kurs, Lehrgang*) will last six weeks, and .... (*während*) that time you will live in the company guesthouse in central London.
Once again, Michael did not know what to say. He didn't hesitate long, he .... (*annehmen*) straight away. That evening, Michael was ever so .... (*aufgeregt*). He lay in his bed and couldn't sleep a wink all night!

Annex A

Alphabetical lists of items for sale in a supermarket

Alphabetisches Verzeichnis der im Supermarkt angebotenen Waren

A.1 Food (general)/Lebensmittel

A.1.1 Alphabetical list English – German

A

almonds	Mandeln
apple sauce	Apfelmus
apricots (dried)	Aprikosen (getrocknet)
apricots (tinned)	Aprikosen (Konserve)

B

baby food	Babynahrung
bacon	Frühstücksspeck
baked beans	gebackene Bohnen (Konserve)
baking powder	Backpulver
barbecue sauce	Grillsoße
beans (dried)	Bohnen (getrocknet)
beef stock cube	Brühwürfel
beetroot (pickled)	Rote Beete (Essigkonserve)
biscuits	Kekse
blancmange powder	Puddingpulver
Bovril	Brotaufstrich (wie Maggi)
brawn (tinned)	Sülze (Fleischkonserve)
Brazil nuts	Paranüsse
breadcrumbs	Paniermehl
brown sugar	brauner Zucker (Rohrzucker)

C

carrots (tinned)	Karotten (Konserve)
cereals	Getreideprodukte (Frühstück)
cheese	Käse
chocolate	Schokolade
cinnamon	Zimt

cocoa powder	Kakaopulver
coconut milk	Kokosmilch
coffee (ground)	Kaffee (gemahlen)
coleslaw	Krautsalat
condensed milk	Dosenmilch
cooking fat	Bratfett (z.B. Biskin)
corned beef	Rindfleischkonserve
cornflakes	Maisflocken
cornflour	Maismehl (entspricht Mondamin)
crabmeat (tinned)	Taschenkrebsfleisch (Konserve)
crackers	Salzkekse
cranberry sauce	Preißelbeersoße
cream	Sahne
crisps	Kartoffelchips
curry paste	Currypaste
curry powder	Currypulver
custard	Vanillesoßenpulver

D

dates (dried)	Datteln (getrocknet)
desicated coconut	Kokosraspeln
dressing	Salatsoße
dumplings (instant)	Kartoffelknödel (Instant)

E

egg	Ei
figs (dried)	Feigen (getrocknet)
flour	Mehl
Frankfurter sausages	Würstchen i. Dose

G

garlic (granulated)	Knoblauchpulver
gherkins	Gewürzgurken
ginger (ground)	Ingwer (gemahlen)
grapefruit (tinned)	Grapefruit (Konserve)
gravy (instant)	Soßenpulver (Instant)
green beans (tinned)	grüne Bohnen (Konserve)

H

hazelnuts	Haselnüsse
herbal infusion	Kräutertee
herring (tinned)	Hering i. Dose
honey	Honig
horseradish	Meerrettich

I

icing sugar	Puderzucker
instant coffee	Instant-Kaffeepulver
instant soup	Tütensuppe

J

jam	Konfitüre
jelly	Gelee, auch: Götterspeise

K

kipper in vegegetabel oil tinned	Bückling in Öl (Konserve)

L

lentils (dried)	Linsen (getrocknet)
lentils (tinned)	Linsen (Konserve)
liquorice	Lakritze

M

malt vinegar	Malzessig (sehr mild)
maple syrup	Ahornsirup
margarine	Margarine
marmalade	Orangenmarmelade
Marmite	Brotaufstrich (wie Maggi)
marshmallows	Marsmallows
mashed potatoes (instant)	Kartoffelpürree (Fertigprodukt)
mayonaise	Majonaise
millet	Hirse
mixed pickles	Essiggemüse
muesli	Müsli

mushrooms (tinned)	Champignons (Konserve)
mustard	Senf

N

noodles	Nudeln
nougat	Nougat
nutmeg	Muskatnuss

O

oatmeal	Haferflocken
olive oil	Olivenöl
olives	Oliven
oranges (tinned)	Orangen (Konserve)
organic food	Bio-Lebensmittel

P

paprika	Paprikapulver
peach (tinned)	Pfirsich (Konserve)
peanut butter	Erdnußbutter
peanuts	Erdnüsse
peas (dried)	Erbsen (getrocknet)
peas (tinned)	Erbsen (Konserve)
pepper	Pfeffer
pickles	Essiggemüse
pineapple (tinned)	Ananas (Konserve)
plums (dried)	Backpflaumen
popcorn	Popcorn
poppy seeds	Mohn
prawns (tinned)	Krabben (Konserve)
preserve	Eingemachtes

R

raisins	Rosinen
rice	Reis
rosemary	Rosmarin

S

salmon (tinned)	Lachs (Konserve)
salt	Salzkekse
sandwich spread	Brotaufstrich (vegetarisch)
sardines in oil	Ölsardinen
semolina	Grieß
sesame seeds	Sesam
shrimps in brine (tinned)	Garnelen (Konserve)
soup (tinned)	Dosensuppe
spaghetti	Spaghetti
spam	Frühstücksfleisch (Konserve)
spices	Gewürze
starch	Stärke
steak & kidney pie	Fleischpastete (Konserve)
suet	Orangeat (Backzutat)
sugar	Zucker
sultanas	Sultaninen (kernlos)
sunflower seeds	Sonneblumenkerne
sweet corn (tinned)	Gemüsemais (Konserve)

T

tapioca	Sago
tartar sauce	Remouladensoße
tea leaves	schwarzer Tee (Blätter)
teabags	schwarzer Tee (Beutel)
toast	Röstbrot
toffee	Sahnebonbons
tomato ketchup	Tomatenketchup
tuna fish (tinned)	Thunfisch (Konserve)

V

vanilla sugar	Vanillezucker
vegetable oil	Pflanzenöl
vegetarian food	vegetarische Lebensmittel
vinegar	Essig

W

walnuts	Walnüsse
wheat flour	Weizenmehl

Y

yeast	Hefe

A.1 Lebensmittel/Food (general)

A.1.2 Alphabetisches Verzeichnis Deutsch – Englisch

A

Ahornsirup	maple syrup
Ananas (Konserve)	pineapple (tinned)
Apfelmus	apple sauce
Aprikosen (getrocknet)	apricots (dried)
Aprikosen (Konserve)	apricots (tinned)

B

Babynahrung	baby food
Backpflaumen	plums (dried)
Backpulver	baking powder
Bio-Lebensmittel	organic food
Bohnen (getrocknet)	beans (dried)
Bratfett (z.B. Biskin)	cooking fat
brauner Zucker (Rohrzucker)	brown sugar
Brotaufstrich (vegetarisch)	sandwich spread
Brotaufstrich (wie Maggi)	Bovril
Brotaufstrich (wie Maggi)	Marmite
Brühwürfel	beef stock cube
Bückling in Öl (Konserve)	kipper in vegegetabel oil (tinned)

C

Champignons (Konserve)	mushrooms (tinned)
Currypaste	curry paste
Currypulver	curry powder

D

Datteln (getrocknet)	dates (dried)
Dosenmilch	condensed milk
Dosensuppe	soup (tinned)

E

Ei	egg
Eingemachtes	preserve
Erbsen (getrocknet)	peas (dried)
Erbsen (Konserve)	peas (tinned)
Erdnußbutter	peanut butter
Erdnüsse	peanuts
Essig	vinegar
Essiggemüse	mixed pickles
Essiggemüse	pickles

F

Feigen (getrocknet)	figs (dried)
Fleischpastete (Konserve)	steak & kidney pie
Frühstücksfleisch (Konserve)	spam
Frühstücksspeck	bacon

G

Garnelen (Konserve)	shrimps in brine (tinned)
gebackene Bohnen (Konserve)	baked beans
Gelee, auch: Götterspeise	jelly
Gemüsemais (Konserve)	sweet corn (tinned)
Getreideprodukte (Frühstück)	cereals
Gewürze	spices
Gewürzgurken	gherkins
Grapefruit (Konserve)	grapefruit (tinned)
Griess	semolina
Grillsoße	barbecue sauce
grüne Bohnen (Konserve)	green beans (tinned)

H

Haferflocken	oatmeal
Haselnüsse	hazelnuts
Hefe	yeast
Hering	herring (tinned)
Hirse	millet
Honig	honey

I

Ingwer (gemahlen)	ginger (ground)
Instant-Kaffeepulver	instant coffee

K

Kaffee (gemahlen)	coffee (ground)
Kakaopulver	cocoa powder
Karotten (Konserve)	carrots (tinned)
Kartoffelchips	crisps
Kartoffelknödel (Instant)	dumplings (instant)
Kartoffelpürree (Fertigprodukt)	mashed potatoes (instant)
Käse	cheese
Kekse	biscuits
Knoblauchpulver	garlic (granulated)
Kokosmilch	coconut milk
Kokosraspeln	desicated coconut
Konfitüre	jam
Krabben (Konserve)	prawns (tinned)
Kräutertee	herbal infusion
Krautsalat	coleslaw

L

Lachs (Konserve)	salmon (tinned)
Lakritze	liquorice
Linsen (getrocknet)	lentils (dried)
Linsen (Konserve)	lentils (tinned)

M

Maisflocken	cornflakes
Maismehl (entspricht Mondamin)	cornflour
Majonaise	mayonaise
Malzessig (sehr mild)	malt vinegar
Mandeln	almonds
Margarine	margarine
Marsmallows	marshmallows
Meerrettich	horseradish
Mehl	flour
Mohn	poppy seeds
Muskatnuss	nutmeg
Müsli	muesli

N

Nougat	nougat
Nudeln	noodles

O

Oliven	olives
Olivenöl	olive oil
Ölsardinen	sardines in oil
Orangeat (Backzutat)	suet
Orangen (Konserve)	oranges (tinned)
Orangenmarmelade	marmalade

P

Paniermehl	breadcrumbs
Paprikapulver	paprika
Paranüsse	Brazil nuts
Pfeffer	pepper
Pfirsich (Konserve)	peach (tinned)
Pflanzenöl	vegetable oil
Popcorn	popcorn
Preißelbeersoße	cranberry sauce
Puddingpulver	blancmange powder

Puderzucker	icing sugar

R

Reis	rice
Remouladensoße	tartar sauce
Rindfleischkonserve	corned beef
Rosinen	raisins
Rosmarin	rosemary
Röstbrot	toast
Rote Beete (Essigkonserve)	beetroot (pickled)

S

Sago	tapioca
Sahne	cream
Sahnebonbons	toffee
Salatsoße	dressing
Salzkekse	crackers
Salzkekse	salt
Schokolade	chocolate
schwarzer Tee (Beutel)	teabags
schwarzer Tee (Blätter)	tea leaves
Senf	mustard
Sesam	sesame seeds
Sonneblumenkerne	sunflower seeds
Soßenpulver (Instant)	gravy (instant)
Spaghetti	spaghetti
Stärke	starch
Sultaninen (kernlos)	sultanas
Sülze (Fleischkonserve)	brawn (tinned)

T

Taschenkrebsfleisch (Konserve)	crabmeat (tinned)
Thunfisch (Konserve)	tuna fish (tinned)
Tomatenketchup	tomato ketchup
Tütensuppe	instant soup

V

Vanillesoßenpulver custard
Vanillezucker vanilla sugar
vegetarische Lebensmittel vegetarian food

W

Walnüsse walnuts
Weizenmehl wheat flour
Würstchen Frankfurter sausages

Z

Zimt cinnamon
Zucker sugar

A.2 Fruits and vegetables/Obst und Gemüse

A

apple Apfel
apricot Aprikose
artichoke Artischoke
asparagus Spargel
avocado Avokado

B

banana Banane
basil Basilikum
bean Bohne
blackcurrant schwarze Johannisbeere
blueberry Blaubeere
Brazil nut Paranuss
broccoli Brokkoli
Brussels sprouts Rosenkohl

C

cabbage Kohl
carrot Möhre
cauliflower Blumenkohl
celery Sellerie
cepe Steinpilz

chanterelle	Pfifferling
cherry	Kirsche
chestnut	Eßkastanie
chili	Chilischote
Chinese cabbage	Chinakohl
chive	Schnittlauch
coconut	Kokosnuss
corn	Mais
corn cob	Maiskolben
cranberry	Preiselbeere
crinkled cabbage	Wirsingkohl
cucumber	Salatgurke

E

eggplant/aubergine	Aubergine
endive	Endiviensalat

F

fennel	Fenchel

G

garlic	Knoblauch
gooseberry	Stachelbeere
grapefruit	Grapefruit
grapes	Weintrauben
green pepper (sweet)	Paprika, grün

H

hazelnut	Haselnuss
honeydew melon	Honigmelone
horseradish	Meerrettich

I

iceberg lettuce	Eisbergsalat

K

kail, kale	Grünkohl

kiwi	Kiwi
kohlrabi	Kohlrabi

L

lamb's lettuce	Feldsalat
leek	Porree
lemon	Zitrone
lime	Limette

M

mango	Mango
marrow	Markkürbis
melon	Melone
mulberry	Maulbeere
mushroom	Champignon

N

nectarine	Nekatrine

O

onion	Zwiebel
orange	Orange, Apfelsine
oregano	Oregano

P

parsley	Petersilie
parsnip	Pastinake
pea	Erbse
peach	Pfirsich
peanut	Erdnuss
pear	Birne
pineapple	Ananas
pistachio	Pistazie
plum	Pflaume
potato	Kartoffel
pumpkin	Kürbis

Q

quince	Quitte

R

raspberry	Himbeere
red cabbage	Rotkohl
redcurrant	rote Johannisbeere
red pepper (sweet)	Paprika, rot
rhubarb	Rhabarber

S

sage	Salbei
salsify	Schwarzwurzel
spinach	Spinat
strawberry	Erdbeere

T

tangerine	Mandarine
thyme	Thymian
tomato	Tomate
turnip	Steckrübe

W

walnut	Walnuss
water cress	Brunnenkresse
white cabbage	Weißkohl
white currant	gelbe Johannisbeeren

Y

yellow pepper (sweet)	Parika, gelb

A.2 Obst und Gemüse/Fruits and vegetables

A

Ananas	pineapple
Apfelsine	orange

Aprikose	apricot
Artischoke	artichoke
Aubergine	eggplant/aubergine
Avokado	avocado

B

Banane	banana
Basilikum	basil
Birne	pear
Blaubeere	blueberry
Blumenkohl	cauliflower
Bohne	bean
Brokkoli	broccoli
Brunnenkresse	water cress

C

Champignon	mushroom
Chilischote	chili
Chinakohl	Chinese cabbage

E

Eisbergsalat	iceberg lettuce
Endiviensalat	endive
Erbse	pea
Erdbeere	strawberry
Erdnuss	peanut
Esskastanie	chestnut

F

Feldsalat	lamb's lettuce
Fenchel	fennel

G

gelbe Johannisbeeren	white currant
Grapefruit	grapefruit
Grünkohl	kail

H

Haselnuss	hazelnut
Himbeere	raspberry
Honigmelone	honeydew melon

K

Kartoffel	potato
Kirsche	cherry
Kiwi	kiwi
Knoblauch	garlic
Kohl	cabbage
Kohlrabi	kohlrabi
Kokosnuss	coconut
Kürbis	pumpkin

L

Limette	lime

M

Mais	corn
Maiskolben	corn cob
Mandarine	tangerine
Mango	mango
Markkürbis	marrow
Maulbeere	mulberry
Meerrettich	horseradish
Melone	melon
Möhre	carrot

N

Nektarine	nectarine

O

Oregano	oregano

P

Paprika, grün	green pepper (sweet)

Paprika, rot	red pepper (sweet)
Paprika, gelb	yellow pepper (sweet)
Paranuss	Brazil nut
Pastinake	parsnip
Petersilie	parsley
Pfifferling	chanterelle
Pfirsich	peach
Pflaume	plum
Pistazie	pistachio
Porree	leek
Preiselbeere	cranberry

Q

Quitte	quince

R

Rhabarber	rhubarb
Rosenkohl	Brussels sprouts
rote Johannisbeere	redcurrant
Rotkohl	red cabbage

S

Salatgurke	cucumber
Salbei	sage
Schnittlauch	chive
schwarze Johannisbeere	blackcurrant
Schwarzwurzel	salsify
Sellerie	celery
Spargel	aspargus
Spinat	spinach
Stachelbeere	gooseberry
Steckrübe	turnip
Steinpilz	cepe

T

Thymian	thyme
Tomate	tomato

W

Walnuss	walnut
Weintraube	grape
Weißkohl	white cabbage
Wirsingkohl	crinkled cabbage

Z

Zitrone	lemon
Zwiebel	onion

A.3 Meat/Fleisch

bacon	Frühstücksspeck
beef	Rindfleisch
black pudding	Blutwurst
brawn	Sülze
breast	Brust
brisket	Rinderbrust
chicken	Hühnchen
chop	Kotelett
cold meat	Aufschnitt
dripping	Schmalz
drumstick	Hähnchenbein, Schlegel
duck	Ente
escalope	Schnitzel
fillet	Filet
gammon	Rohschinken
goose	Gans
guinea fowl	Perlhuhn
ham	gekochter Schinken
hare	Hase
joint	Bratenstück
joint of beef	Rinderbraten
joint of pork	Schweinebraten
kidney	Niere
lamb	Lammfleisch
lard	fetter Speck

leg	Keule
liver	Leber
minced meat	Hackfleisch
mutton	Hammelfleisch
oxtail	Ochsenschwanz
partridge	Rebhuhn
pate	Leberwurst
pigeon	Taube
pork	Schweinefleisch
poultry	Geflügel
rabbit	Kaninchen
sausage	Bratwürstchen
sirloin, tenderloin	Lende
steak	Steak
steak	Rindfleisch zum Kurzbraten
sweetbreads	Kalbsbries
tongue	Zunge
trotter	Haxe
turkey	Truthahn, Puter
veal	Kalbfleisch
venison	Wild
wild boar	Wildschwein

A.3 Fleisch/Meat

Aufschnitt	cold meat
Blutwurst	black pudding
Bratenstück	joint
Bratwürstchen	sausage
Brust	breast
Ente	duck
fetter Speck	lard
Filet	fillet
Frühstücksspeck	bacon
Gans	goose
Geflügel	poultry
gekochter Schinken	ham

Hackfleisch	minced meat
Hähnchenbein, Schlegel	drumstick
Hammelfleisch	mutton
Hase	hare
Haxe	trotter
Hühnchen	chicken
Kalbfleisch	veal
Kalbsbries	sweetbreads
Kaninchen	rabbit
Keule	leg
Kotelett	chop
Lammfleisch	lamb
Leber	liver
Leberwurst	pate
Lende	sirloin, tenderloin
Niere	kidney
Ochsenschwanz	oxtail
Perlhuhn	guinea fowl
Rebhuhn	partridge
Rinderbraten	joint of beef
Rinderbrust	brisket
Rindfleisch	beef
Rindfleisch zum Kurzbraten	steak
Rohschinken	gammon
Schmalz	dripping
Schnitzel	escalope
Schweinebraten	joint of pork
Schweinefleisch	pork
Steak	steak
Sülze	brawn
Taube	pigeon
Truthahn, Puter	turkey
Wild	venison
Wildschwein	wild boar
Zunge	tongue

A.4 Dairy products/Molkereiprodukte

blue cheese	Schimmelkäse
butter	Butter
buttermilk	Buttermilch
cheese	Käse
cottage cheese	Frischkäse
cream	Sahne
curd	Quark
hard cheese	Hartkäse
milk	Milch
rice pudding	Milchreis
skimmed milk	Magermilch
soft cheese	Weichkäse
sour cream	Saure Sahne, Schmand
whipped cream	Schlagsahne
yoghurt	Joghurt

A.4 Molkereiprodukte/Dairy products

Butter	butter
Buttermilch	buttermilk
Frischkäse	cottage cheese
Hartkäse	hard cheese
Joghurt	yoghurt
Käse	cheese
Magermilch	skimmed milk
Milch	milk
Milchreis	rice pudding
Quark	curd
Sahne	cream
Saure Sahne, Schmand	sour cream
Schimmelkäse	blue cheese
Schlagsahne	whipped cream
Weichkäse	soft cheese

A.5 Bakery products/Backwaren

apple pie	Apfelstrudel
barley bread	Gerstenbrot
biscuit	Keks, Plätzchen
Black Forest gateau	Schwarzwälder Kirschtorte
bread	Brot
brown bread	dunkles Brot
cake	Kuchen
cookie	Keks, Plätzchen
French loaf	Baguette
loaf	Brotlaib
muffin	Hefeteigkuchen
roll	Brötchen
rusk	Zwieback
rye bread	Roggenbrot
slice	Scheibe
tart	Obstkuchen
toast	Röstbrot
white bread	Weißbrot
wholemeal bread	Vollkornbrot

A.5 Backwaren/Bakery products

Apfelstrudel	apple pie
Baguette	French loaf
Brot	bread
Brötchen	roll
Brotlaib	loaf
dunkles Brot	brown bread
Gerstenbrot	barley bread
Hefeteigkuchen	muffin
Keks, Plätzchen	biscuit
Keks, Plätzchen	cookie
Kuchen	cake
Obstkuchen	tart
Roggenbrot	rye bread

Röstbrot	toast
Scheibe	slice
Schwarzwälder Kirschtorte	Black Forest gateau
Vollkornbrot	wholemeal bread
Weißbrot	white bread
Zwieback	rusk

A.6 Frozen food/Tiefkühlkost

beef steak	Rindersteak
Black Forest gateau	Schwarzwälder Kirschtorte
chips	Pommes Frites
dough	Teig
dumplings	Klöße
fisch fillet	Fischfilet
fish fingers	Fischstäbchen
fruit	Obst
herbs	Kräuter
ice cream	Speiseeis
lamb	Lamm
orange juice	Orangensaft
pizza	Pizza
poultry	Geflügel
rolls	Brötchen
sausages	Bratwürstchen
shellfish	Schalentiere (Krabben etc.)
vegetables	Gemüse

A.6 Tiefkühlkost/Frozen food

Bratwürstchen	sausages
Brötchen	rolls
Fischfilet	fisch fillet
Fischstäbchen	fish fingers
Geflügel	poultry
Gemüse	vegetables
Klöße	dumplings

Kräuter	herbs
Lamm	lamb
Obst	fruit
Orangensaft	orange juice
Pizza	pizza
Pommes Frites	chips
Rindersteak	beef steak
Schalentiere (Krabben etc.)	shellfish
Schwarzwälder Kirschtorte	Black Forest gateau
Speiseeis	ice cream
Teig	dough

A.7 Fish and seafood/Fisch und Meeresfrüchte

barbel	Barbe
carp	Karpfen
catfish	Wels
char	Saibling
clam	Venusmuschel
coalfish	Köhler, Seelachs
cockle	Herzmuschel
cod	Kabeljau
crab	Taschenkrebs
crawfish	Languste
crayfish	Flußkrebs
eel	Aal
fillet	Filet
fishbone	Gräte
greyling	Äsche
haddock	Schellfisch
halibut	Heilbutt
herring	Hering
jellied eel	Aal in Gelee
kipper	Bückling
lobster	Hummer
mackerel	Makrele
monkfisch	Seeteufel

mussels	Miesmuscheln
oyster	Auster
perch	Barsch
pike	Hecht
pikeperch	Zander
plaice	Scholle
prawn	Garnele
ray	Rochen
red mullet	Rotbarbe
roach	Plötze, Rotauge
roe	Rogen
salmon	Lachs
scallop	Jakobsmuschel
shark	Hai
shellfish	Schalentier
shrimps	Crevetten
smoked	geräuchert
sole	Seezunge
sprat	Sprotte
squid	Tintenfisch
sturgeon	Stör
tench	Schleie
trout	Forelle
tuna fish, tunny	Thunfisch

A.7 Fisch und Meeresfrüchte/Fish and seafood

Aal	eel
Aal in Gelee	jellied eel
Äsche	greyling
Auster	oyster
Barbe	barbel
Barsch	perch
Bückling	kipper
Crevetten	shrimps
Filet	fillet
Flußkrebs	crayfish

Forelle	trout
Garnele	prawn
geräuchert	smoked
Gräte	fishbone
Hai	shark
Hecht	pike
Heilbutt	halibut
Hering	herring
Herzmuschel	cockle
Hummer	lobster
Jakobsmuschel	scallop
Kabeljau	cod
Karpfen	carp
Köhler, Seelachs	coalfish
Lachs	salmon
Languste	crawfish
Makrele	mackerel
Miesmuscheln	mussels
Plötze, Rotauge	roach
Rochen	ray
Rogen	roe
Rotbarbe	red mullet
Saibling	char
Schalentier	shellfish
Schellfisch	haddock
Schleie	tench
Scholle	plaice
Seeteufel	monkfisch
Seezunge	sole
Sprotte	sprat
Stör	sturgeon
Taschenkrebs	crab
Thunfisch	tuna fish, tunny
Tintenfisch	squid
Venusmuschel	clam
Wels	catfish
Zander	pikeperch

A.8 Stationery/Bürobedarf

ball point pen	Kugelschreiber
biro	Kugelschreiber (U)
calendar	Kalender
cardboard	Pappe
crayon	Buntstift
diary	Terminkalender
drawing pin	Heftzwecke
elastic band	Gummiband
envelope	Briefumschlag
felt pen	Filzstift
fountain pen	Füllfederhalter
glue	Klebstoff
ink	Tinte
ink cartridge	Tintenpatrone
inkpad	Stempelkissen
pair of scissors	Schere
paper	Papier
paperclip	Büroklammer
pen	Stift
pencil sharpener	Anspitzer
pocket calculator	Taschenrechner
protractor	Winkelmesser
punch	Locher
rubber	Radiergummi
ruler	Lineal
sellotape	Tesafilm
staple	Heftklammer
stapler	Heftmaschine, Tacker
textmarker	Textmarker
tray	Ablagekorb
writing pad	Schreibblock

A.8 Bürobedarf/Stationery

Ablagekorb	tray
Anspitzer	pencil sharpener

Briefumschlag	envelope
Buntstift	crayon
Büroklammer	paperclip
Filzstift	felt pen
Füllfederhalter	fountain pen
Gummiband	elastic band
Heftklammer	staple
Heftmaschine, Tacker	stapler
Heftzwecke	drawing pin
Kalender	calendar
Klebstoff	glue
Kugelschreiber	ball point pen
Kugelschreiber (U)	biro
Lineal	ruler
Locher	punch
Papier	paper
Pappe	cardboard
Radiergummi	rubber
Schere	pair of scissors
Schreibblock	writing pad
Stempelkissen	inkpad
Stift	pen
Taschenrechner	pocket calculator
Terminkalender	diary
Tesafilm	sellotape
Textmarker	textmarker
Tinte	ink
Tintenpatrone	ink cartridge
Winkelmesser	protractor

A.9 Haberdashery/Kurzwaren

button	Knopf
chalk	Schneiderkreide
circular needle	Rundstricknadel
cotton	Nähgarn
crochet hook	Häkelnadel

eyelet	Öse
hook	Haken
hoop	Stickrahmen
knitting needle	Stricknadel
needle	Nähnadel
pair of scissors	Schere
pattern	Schnittmuster
pin	Stecknadel
pin cushion	Nadelkissen
pinking shears	Zickzackschere
press stud	Druckknopf
safety pin	Sicherheitsnadel
shoulder pad	Schulterpolster
spool of thread	Rolle Nähgarn
tape measure	Maßband
thimble	Fingerhut
Vortex fastener	Klettverschluss
wheel	Rädchen
zip	Reißverschluss

A.9 Kurzwaren/Haberdashery

Druckknopf	press stud
Fingerhut	thimble
Häkelnadel	crochet hook
Haken	hook
Klettverschluss	Vortex fastener
Knopf	button
Maßband	tape measure
Nadelkissen	pin cushion
Nähgarn	cotton
Nähnadel	needle
Öse	eyelet
Rädchen	wheel
Reißverschluss	zip
Rolle Nähgarn	spool of thread
Rundstricknadel	circular needle

Schere	pair of scissors
Schneiderkreide	chalk
Schnittmuster	pattern
Schulterpolster	shoulder pad
Sicherheitsnadel	safety pin
Stecknadel	pin
Stickrahmen	hoop
Stricknadel	knitting needle
Zickzackschere	pinking shears

A.10 Kitchen utensils/Haushaltswaren

adhesive tape	Klebeband
baking sheet	Backblech
baking tin	Kuchenform
battery	Batterie
biscuit cutters	Ausstechformen
bottle opener	Flaschenöffner
brush	Handfeger
bulb	Glühbirne
candle	Kerze
cleaver	Küchenbeil
cooking spoon	Kochlöffel
cork screw	Korkenzieher
cup	Tasse
cutting board	Schneidebrett
dust bag	Staubsaugerbeutel
dustpan	Kehrblech
egg slicer	Eierschneider
egg timer	Eieruhr
fluorescent lamp	Leuchtstoffröhre
fork	Gabel
frying pan	Bratpfanne
funnel	Trichter
fuse	Sicherung
garlic press	Knoblauchpresse
glue	Klebstoff

grater	Reibe
gravy ladle	Soßenkelle
kitchen scale	Küchenwaage
kitchen timer	Küchenuhr
knife	Messer
ladle	Schöpflöffel
lemon squeezer	Zitronenpresse
lid	Topfdeckel
lighter	Feuerzeug
matches	Streichhölzer
measuring jug	Meßbecher
mesh strainer	Passiersieb
nutcracker	Nußknacker
pair of scissors	Schere
pot	Kochtopf
potato masher	Kartoffelstampfer
poultry shears	Geflügelschere
pressure cooker	Schnellkochtopf
rolling pin	Nudelholz
rubber band	Gummiring
rubber seal	Weckring
salad spinner	Salatschleuder
saucepan	Stieltopf
saucer	Untertasse
screwdriver	Schraubenzieher
skimmer	Schaumkelle
slice	Pfannenwender
string	Bindfaden
tablespoon	Eßlöffel
tack	Heftzwecke
teaspoon	Teelöffel
thermometer	Thermometer
tin foil	Alufolie
tin opener	Dosenöffner
whisk	Schneebesen

A.10 Haushaltswaren/Kitchen utensils

Alufolie	tin foil
Ausstechformen	biscuit cutters
Backblech	baking sheet
Batterie	battery
Bindfaden	string
Bratpfanne	frying pan
Dosenöffner	tin opener
Eierschneider	egg slicer
Eieruhr	egg timer
Eßlöffel	tablespoon
Feuerzeug	lighter
Flaschenöffner	bottle opener
Gabel	fork
Geflügelschere	poultry shears
Glühbirne	bulb
Gummiring	rubber band
Handfeger	brush
Heftzwecke	tack
Kartoffelstampfer	potato masher
Kehrblech	dustpan
Kerze	candle
Klebeband	adhesive tape
Klebstoff	glue
Knoblauchpresse	garlic press
Kochlöffel	cooking spoon
Kochtopf	pot
Korkenzieher	cork screw
Küchenbeil	cleaver
Kuchenform	baking tin
Küchenuhr	kitchen timer
Küchenwaage	kitchen scale
Leuchtstoffröhre	fluorescent lamp
Meßbecher	measuring jug
Messer	knife
Nudelholz	rolling pin

Nußknacker	nutcracker
Passiersieb	mesh strainer
Pfannenwender	slice
Reibe	grater
Salatschleuder	salad spinner
Schaumkelle	skimmer
Schere	pair of scissors
Schneebesen	whisk
Schneidebrett	cutting board
Schnellkochtopf	pressure cooker
Schöpflöffel	ladle
Schraubenzieher	screwdriver
Sicherung	fuse
Soßenkelle	gravy ladle
Staubsaugerbeutel	dust bag
Stieltopf	saucepan
Streichhölzer	matches
Tasse	cup
Teelöffel	teaspoon
Thermometer	thermometer
Topfdeckel	lid
Trichter	funnel
Untertasse	saucer
Weckring	rubber seal
Zitronenpresse	lemon squeezer

A.11 Flowers/Blumen

azalea	Azalee
begonia	Begonie
bunch	Strauß
busy lizzy	Fleißiges Lieschen
buttercup	Butterblume
carnation	Nelke
crocus	Krokus
dafodil	Narzisse, Osterglocke
dahlia	Dahlie

daisy	Margerite
flowerpot	Blumentopf
fusia	Fuchsie
geranium	Geranie
gerbera	Gerbera
gladiolus	Gladiole
Interflora	Fleurop
iris	Iris
leaf	Blatt
lily	Lilie
lily-of-the-valley	Maiglöckchen
Michaelmas daisy	Aster
orchid	Orchidee
peony	Pfingstrose
rose	Rose
snowdrop	Schneeglöckchen
snowflake	Märzenbecher
stem	Stiel
stepmother	Stiefmütterchen
stocks	Levkojen
sunflower	Sonnenblume
tulip	Tulpe
vase	Blumenvase
violet	Veilchen
wreath	Kranz

A.11 Blumen/Flowers

Azalee	azalea
Begonie	begonia
Blatt	leaf
Blumentopf	flowerpot
Blumenvase	vase
Butterblume	buttercup
Dahlie	dahlia
Fleißiges Lieschen	busy lizzy
Fleurop	Interflora

Fuchsie	fusia
Geranie	geranium
Gerbera	gerbera
Gladiole	gladiolus
Iris	iris
Kranz	wreath
Krokus	crocus
Levkojen	stocks
Lilie	lily
Maiglöckchen	lily-of-the-valley
Margerite	daisy
Märzenbecher	snowflake
Narzisse, Osterglocke	dafodil
Nelke	carnation
Orchidee	orchid
Pfingstrose	peony
Rose	rose
Schneeglöckchen	snowdrop
Sonnenblume	sunflower
Stiefmütterchen	stepmother
Stiel	stem
Strauß	bunch
Tulpe	tulip
Veilchen	violet

A.12 Chemistry/Drogerieartikel

blusher	Rouge
brush	Bürste
comb	Kamm
cotton bud	Wattestäbchen (Q-Tips)
cotton wool	Watte
curler	Lockenwickler
deodorant	Deo
dish washer cleanser	Spülmaschinenreiniger
dishcloth	Geschirrspültuch
disposable	Einweg

dummy	Schnuller
eye shadow	Lidschatten
eyeliner	Lidstift
fabric softener	Weichspüler
feeding bottle	Babyfläschchen
flannel	Waschlappen
glove	Handschuh
hair dye	Haarfärbemittel
hair spray	Haarspray
hanky (U)	Papiertaschentuch
lipstick	Lippenstift
liquid soap	Flüssigseife
napkin	Windel
night cream	Nachtcreme
pair of tweezers	Pinzette
panty liner	Slipeinlage
paper handkerchief, tissue	Papiertaschentuch
perfume	Parfüm
powder	Puder
shampoo	Haarwaschmittel
shoe polish	Schuhcreme
shower gel	Duschgel
skin cream	Hautcreme
soap	Seife
sponge	Schwamm
tampon	Tampon
toilet paper	Toilettenpapier
toothbrush	Zahnbürste
toothpaste	Zahnpasta
toothpick	Zahnstocher
washing powder	Waschpulver
washing-up liquid	Geschirrspülmittel

A.12 Drogerieartikel/Chemistry

Babyfläschchen	feeding bottle
Bürste	brush

Deo	deodorant
Duschgel	shower gel
Einweg	disposable
Flüssigseife	liquid soap
Geschirrspülmittel	washing-up liquid
Geschirrspültuch	dishcloth
Haarfärbemittel	hair dye
Haarspray	hair spray
Haarwaschmittel	shampoo
Handschuh	glove
Hautcreme	skin cream
Kamm	comb
Lidschatten	eye shadow
Lidstift	eyeliner
Lippenstift	lipstick
Lockenwickler	curler
Nachtcreme	night cream
Papiertaschentuch	hanky (U)
Papiertaschentuch	paper handkerchief, tissue
Parfüm	perfume
Pinzette	pair of tweezers
Puder	powder
Rouge	blusher
Schnuller	dummy
Schuhcreme	shoe polish
Schwamm	sponge
Seife	soap
Slipeinlage	panty liner
Spülmaschinenreiniger	dish washer cleanser
Tampon	tampon
Toilettenpapier	toilet paper
Waschlappen	flannel
Waschpulver	washing powder
Watte	cotton wool
Wattestäbchen (Q-Tips)	cotton bud
Weichspüler	fabric softener
Windel	napkin

Zahnbürste	toothbrush
Zahnpasta	toothpaste
Zahnstocher	toothpick

A.13 Drinks/Getränke

ale	leichtes helles Bier
Babycham	Birnenschaumwein
beer	Bier
bitter	obergärige Biersorte
bitters	Magenbitter
blackcurrant juice	schwarzer Johannisbeersaft
brandy	Weinbrand
champagne	Champagner
cider	Apfelwein
Coke	Coca-Cola
Drambuie	schottischer Whiskylikör
fruit juice	Fruchtsaft
gin	Gin
ginger ale	Ingwerbier
grape juice	Traubensaft
grapefruit juice	Grapefruit-Saft
Hock	Rheinwein
lager	untergäriges helles Bier
lemon juice	Zitronensaft
lemonade	Limonade
liqueur	Likör
mild	obergärige Biersorte (mild)
milk stout	Malzbier
mineral water	Mineralwasser
orange juice	Orangensaft
port	Portwein
red wine	Rotwein
rum	Rum
scrumpy	Apfelmost (stark)
shandy	Alster

sherry	Sherry
soda water	Sodawasser
sparkling water	Wasser mit Kohlensäure
sparkling wine	Sekt
spirits	Spirituosen
Sprite	Sprite
still water	Mineralwasser ohne Kohlensäure
stout	dunkles Starkbier
syrup	Sirup
table water	Tafelwasser
table wine	Tischwein
tomato juice	Tomatensaft
tonic water	Tonic
vodka	Wodka
whiskey	irischer/Am. Whiskey
whisky	schottischer Whisky
white wine	Weißwein
wine	Wein

A.13 Getränke/Drinks

Alster	shandy
Apfelmost (stark)	scrumpy
Apfelwein	cider
Bier	beer
Birnenschaumwein	Babycham
Champagner	champagne
Coca-Cola	Coke
dunkles Starkbier	stout
Fruchtsaft	fruit juice
Gin	gin
Grapefruit-Saft	grapefruit juice
Ingwerbier	ginger ale
irischer/Am. Whiskey	whiskey
leichtes helles Bier	ale
Likör	liqueur

Limonade	lemonade
Magenbitter	bitters
Malzbier	milk stout
Mineralwasser	mineral water
Mineralwasser ohne Kohlen-säure	still water
obergärige Biersorte	bitter
obergärige Biersorte (mild)	mild
Orangensaft	orange juice
Portwein	port
Rheinwein	Hock
Rotwein	red wine
Rum	rum
schottischer Whisky	whisky
schottischer Whiskylikör	Drambuie
schwarzer Johannisbeersaft	blackcurrant juice
Sekt	sparkling wine
Sherry	sherry
Sirup	syrup
Sodawasser	soda water
Spirituosen	spirits
Sprite	Sprite
Tafelwasser	table water
Tischwein	table wine
Tomatensaft	tomato juice
Tonic	tonic water
Traubensaft	grape juice
untergäriges helles Bier	lager
Wasser mit Kohlensäure	sparkling water
Wein	wine
Weinbrand	brandy
Weißwein	white wine
Wodka	vodka
Zitronensaft	lemon juice

Annex B

List of irregular verbs

ABC der unregelmäßigen Verben

(Das Zeichen * bedeutet, dass auch die regelmäßige Form gebräuchlich ist.)

Die Bezeichnung „unregelmäßig bei Verben“ bedeutet, dass die Formen des „simple past“ und des „perfect (present perfect und past perfect)“ nicht durch Anhängen von „-ed“ an die Grundform des Verbs sondern auf unregelmäßige Art gebildet werden.

I	ich	1. Person Einzahl
you	du	2. Person Einzahl
he	er	3. Person Einzahl männlich
she	sie	3. Person Einzahl weiblich
it	es	3. Person Einzahl sächlich
we	wir	1. Person Mehrzahl
you	ihr	2. Person Mehrzahl
they	sie	3. Person Mehrzahl

Hilfsverben

present/ Gegenwart	simple past/ Vergangenheit	present perfect/ vollendete Gegenwart	deutsche Bedeutung
to **be**	was/were	have been	sein
to **have**	had	have had	haben
to **do**	did	have done	tun
to **make**	made	have made	machen

Vollverben

to **arise**	arose	have arisen	entstehen
to **bear**	bore	have borne	tragen (auch: ertragen)
to **beat**	beat	have beaten	schlagen (z.B. Trommel)
to **become**	became	have become	werden
to **begin**	began	have begun	anfangen
to **bend**	bent	have bent	biegen

to **bet**	bet	have bet	wetten
to **bid**	bid	have bid	bieten
to **bind**	bound	have bound	binden
to **bite**	bit	have bitten	beißen
to **bleed**	bled	have bled	bluten
to **blow**	blew	have blown	blasen
to **break**	broke	have broken	zerbrechen
to **bring**	brought	have brought	herbringen
to **broadcast**	broadcast	have broadcast	senden (Funk)
to **build**	built	have built	bauen
to **burn**	burnt	have burnt	brennen, verbrennen
to **burst**	burst	have burst	platzen
to **buy**	bought	have bought	kaufen
to **catch**	caught	have caught	fangen
to **choose**	chose	have chosen	auswählen
to **come**	came	have come	kommen
to **cost**	cost	have cost	kosten
to **creep**	crept	have crept	schleichen
to **cut**	cut	have cut	schneiden
to **deal**	dealt	have dealt	mit etwas befassen
to **dig**	dug	have dug	graben
to **draw**	drew	have drawn	ziehen (auch: zeichnen)
to **dream**	dreamt*	have dreamt	träumen
to **drink**	drank	have drunk	trinken
to **drive**	drove	have driven	fahren
to **eat**	ate	have eaten	essen
to **fall**	fell	have fallen	fallen
to **feed**	fed	have fed	füttern
to **feel**	felt	have felt	(sich) fühlen
to **fight**	fought	have fought	kämpfen
to **find**	found	have found	finden
to **flee**	fled	have fled	fliehen
to **fly**	flew	have flown	fliegen
to **forbid**	forbade	have forbidden	verbieten

to **forget**	forgot	have forgotten	vergessen
to **forgive**	forgave	have forgiven	vergeben, verzeihen
to **freeze**	froze	have frozen	gefrieren
to **get**	got	have got	bekommen
to **give**	gave	have given	geben
to **go**	went	have gone	gehen
to **grind**	ground	have ground	mahlen, schleifen
to **grow**	grew	have grown	wachsen (auch: anbauen)
to **hang**	hung	have hung	aufhängen
to **hear**	heard	have heard	hören
to **hide**	hid	have hidden	verstecken
to **hit**	hit	have hit	treffen (Ziel)
to **hold**	held	have held	halten
to **hurt**	hurt	have hurt	wehtun, schmerzen
to **keep**	kept	have kept	halten (z.B. Haustier)
to **know**	knew	have known	wissen, kennen
to **lay**	laid	have laid	etwas hinlegen
to **lead**	led	have led	leiten, führen
to **leap**	leapt	have leapt	hüpfen
to **lean**	lent	have lent	anlehnen, herauslehnen
to **learn**	learnt*	have learnt	lernen
to **leave**	left	have left	verlassen
to **lend**	lent	have lent	verleihen
to **let**	let	have let	lassen (auch: vermieten)
to **lie**	lay	have lain	liegen (z.B. im Bett)
to **light**	lit*	have lit	anzünden
to **lose**	lost	have lost	verlieren
to **make**	made	have made	machen
to **mean**	meant	have meant	meinen, bedeuten
to **meet**	met	have met	treffen (jmd. antreffen

to **pay**	paid	have paid	bezahlen
to **put**	put	have put	setzen, stellen, legen
to **read**	read	have read	lesen
to **ride**	rode	have ridden	reiten
to **ring**	rang	have rung	klingeln, läuten
to **rise**	rose	have risen	aufgehen
to **run**	ran	have run	rennen
to **saw**	sawed	have sawn	sägen
to **say**	said	have said	sagen
to **see**	saw	have seen	sehen
to **seek**	sought	have sought	suchen
to **sell**	sold	have sold	verkaufen
to **send**	sent	have sent	senden, schicken
to **set**	set	have set	setzen, aufstellen
to **sew**	sewed	have sewn	nähen
to **shake**	shook	have shaken	schütteln
to **sew**	sewed	have sewn	nähen
to **shine**	shone	have shone	scheinen, glänzen
to **shoot**	shot	have shot	schießen
to **show**	showed	have shown	zeigen
to **shrink**	shrank	have shrunk	schrumpfen, einlaufen
to **shut**	shut	have shut	schließen
to **sing**	sang	have sung	singen
to **sink**	sank	have sunk	sinken, versenken
to **sit**	sat	have sat	sitzen
to **sleep**	slept	have slept	schlafen
to **smell**	smelt*	have smelt	riechen
to **speak**	spoke	have spoken	sprechen
to **spell**	spelt*	have spelt	buchstabieren
to **spend**	spent	have spent	Geld ausgeben, auch: Zeit verbringen
to **spill**	spilt	have spilt	verschütten
to **spit**	spat	have spat	spucken
to **split**	split	have split	spalten
to **spoil**	spoilt	have spoilt	verderben
to **spread**	spread	have spread	ausbreiten

to **spring**	sprang	have sprung	springen
to **stand**	stood	have stood	stehen
to **steal**	stole	have stolen	stehlen
to **stick**	stuck	have stuck	anstecken, ankleben
to **sting**	stung	have stung	stechen
to **stink**	stank	have stunk	stinken
to **strike**	struck	have struck	zuschlagen (auch: prägen)
to **swear**	swore	have sworn	schwören (auch: fluchen)
to **sweep**	swept	have swept	fegen
to **swim**	swam	have swum	schwimmen
to **swing**	swung	have swung	schwingen
to **take**	took	have taken	nehmen
to **teach**	taught	have taught	lehren, unterrichten
to **tear**	tore	have torn	zerreißen
to **tell**	told	have told	erzählen
to **think**	thought	have thought	denken
to **throw**	threw	have thrown	werfen
to **tread**	trod	have trodden	trampeln, austreten
to **understand**	understood	have understood	verstehen
to **wear**	wore	have worn	tragen v. Kleidung
to **weave**	wove	have woven	weben
to **weep**	wept	have wept	weinen
to **win**	won	have won	gewinnen
to **wind**	wound	have wound	aufziehen (z.B. Uhr)
to **write**	wrote	have written	schreiben

ABC der unregelmäßigen Verben II

(Das Zeichen * bedeutet, daß auch die regelmäßige Form gebräuchlich ist.)

Teil 2: Einteilung der Verben in Gruppen

Unregelmäßige Verben sind nicht vollkommen unregelmäßig, sondern sie folgen meist ebenfalls bestimmten Regelmäßigkeiten innerhalb ihrer Gruppe. Wenn man sie nach Gruppen lernt, dann geht das erheblich einfacher als wenn man sie nach alphabetischer Reihenfolge lernt.

In dieser Gruppe sind die Verben in allen drei Zeiten (present, simple past und present perfect) gleich:

to **bet**	bet	have bet	wetten
to **bid**	bid	have bid	bieten
to **broadcast**	broadcast	have broadcast	senden (Funk)
to **burst**	burst	have burst	platzen
to **cost**	cost	have cost	kosten
to **cut**	cut	have cut	schneiden
to **hit**	hit	have hit	treffen (Ziel)
to **hurt**	hurt	have hurt	wehtun, schmerzen
to **let**	let	have let	lassen (auch: vermieten)
to **put**	put	have put	setzen, stellen, legen
to **read**	read	have read	lesen
to **set**	set	have set	setzen, aufstellen
to **split**	split	have split	spalten
to **spread**	spread	have spread	ausbreiten
to **shut**	shut	have shut	schließen

In dieser Gruppe besteht zwischen den Formen des Verbs in der Zeit „present" und den beiden weiteren Formen des Verbs in den Zeiten „simple past" und „present perfect" ein Unterschied, aber die beiden letzten Formen sind gleich, und auch diese Verben lassen sich in mehrere Gruppen einteilen, für die jeweils dieselben Regelmäßigkeiten gelten:

to **bend**	bent	have bent	biegen
to **build**	built	have built	bauen
to **lend**	lent	have lent	verleihen
to **send**	sent	have sent	senden, schicken
to **spend**	spent	have spent	Geld ausgeben, auch: Zeit verbringen

to **creep**	crept	have crept	schleichen
to **feel**	felt	have felt	(sich) fühlen
to **keep**	kept	have kept	halten (z.B. Haustier)
to **sleep**	slept	have slept	schlafen
to **sweep**	swept	have swept	fegen
to **weep**	wept	have wept	weinen
to **lean**	lent	have lent	anlehnen, herauslehnen
to **leap**	lept	have lept	hüpfen
to **spell**	spelt*	have spelt	buchstabieren

to **spill**	spilt	have spilt	verschütten
to **smell**	smelt*	have smelt	riechen
to **burn**	burnt	have burnt	brennen, verbrennen
to **learn**	learnt*	have learnt	lernen
to **mean**	meant	have meant	meinen, bedeuten
to **spoil**	spoilt	have spoilt	verderben
to **deal**	dealt	have dealt	mit etwas befassen
to **bring**	brought	have brought	herbringen
to **buy**	bought	have bought	kaufen
to **fight**	fought	have fought	kämpfen
to **think**	thought	have thought	denken
to **seek**	sought	have sought	suchen
to **bind**	bound	have bound	binden
to **find**	found	have found	finden
to **grind**	ground	have ground	mahlen, schleifen
to **wind**	wound	have wound	aufziehen
to **sell**	sold	have sold	verkaufen
to **tell**	told	have told	erzählen
to **stand**	stood	have stood	stehen
to **understand**	understood	have understood	verstehen
to **feed**	fed	have fed	füttern
to **flee**	fled	have fled	fliehen
to **meet**	met	have met	treffen (jmd. antreffen
to **leave**	left	have left	verlassen
to **pay**	paid	have paid	bezahlen
to **say**	said	have said	sagen
to **lay**	laid	have laid	etwas hinlegen
to **dig**	dug	have dug	graben
to **hang**	hung	have hung	aufhängen
to **catch**	caught	have caught	fangen
to **deal** in sth.	dealt	have dealt	mit etwas handeln

to **dream**	dreamt*	have dreamt	träumen
to **get**	got	have got	bekommen
to **hear**	heard	have heard	hören
to **hold**	held	have held	halten
to **lead**	led	have led	leiten, führen
to **light**	lit*	have lit	anzünden
to **lose**	lost	have lost	verlieren
to **make**	made	have made	machen
to **shine**	shone	have shone	scheinen, glänzen
to **shoot**	shot	have shot	schießen
to **sit**	sat	have sat	sitzen
to **spit**	spat	have spat	spucken
to **stick**	stuck	have stuck	anstecken, ankleben
to **sting**	stung	have stung	stechen
to **swing**	swung	have swung	schwingen
to **strike**	struck	have struck	zuschlagen (auch: prägen)
to **teach**	taught	have taught	lehren, unterrichten
to **win**	won	have won	gewinnen

In dieser Gruppe besteht zwischen den Formen des Verbs in den Zeiten „present", „simple past" und „present perfect" jeweils ein Unterschied, wobei aber auch diese Verben innerhalb ihrer Gruppen Regelmäßigkeiten folgen:

to **bear**	bore	have born	tragen (auch: ertragen)
to **swear**	swore	have sworn	schwören (auch: fluchen)
to **tear**	tore	have torn	zerreißen
to **wear**	wore	have worn	tragen (Kleidung)
to **blow**	blew	have blown	blasen
to **fly**	flew	have flown	fliegen
to **know**	knew	have known	wissen, kennen
to **grow**	grew	have grown	wachsen (auch: anbauen)
to **throw**	threw	have thrown	werfen
to **draw**	drew	have drawn	ziehen (auch: zeichnen)
to **become**	became	have become	werden
to **come**	came	have come	kommen

to **shake**	shook	have shaken	schütteln
to **take**	took	have taken	nehmen
to **begin**	began	have begun	anfangen
to **ring**	rang	have rung	klingeln, läuten
to **sing**	sang	have sung	singen
to **swim**	swam	have swum	schwimmen
to **stink**	stank	have stunk	stinken
to **drink**	drank	have drunk	trinken
to **shrink**	shrank	have shrunk	schrumpfen, einlaufen
to **sink**	sank	have sunk	sinken, versenken
to **spring**	sprang	have sprung	springen
to **forbid**	forbade	have forbidden	verbieten
to **forgive**	forgave	have forgiven	vergeben, verzeihen
to **give**	gave	have given	geben
to **break**	broke	have broken	zerbrechen
to **speak**	spoke	have spoken	sprechen
to **wake**	woke	have woken	wecken
to **weave**	wove	have woven	weben
to **steal**	stole	have stolen	stehlen
to **bite**	bit	have bitten	beißen
to **hide**	hid	have hidden	verstecken
to **drive**	drove	have driven	fahren (Kfz führen)
to **ride**	rode	have ridden	reiten
to **write**	wrote	have written	schreiben
to **saw**	sawed	have sawn	sägen
to **show**	showed	have shown	zeigen
to **arise**	arose	have arisen	entstehen
to **rise**	rose	have risen	aufgehen
to **beat**	beat	have beaten	schlagen (z.B. Trommel)
to **choose**	chose	have chosen	auswählen
to **eat**	ate	have eaten	essen

to **fall**	fell	have fallen	fallen
to **forget**	forgot	have forgotten	vergessen
to **freeze**	froze	have frozen	gefrieren
to **go**	went	have gone	gehen
to **lie**	lay	have lain	liegen (z.B. im Bett)
to **run**	ran	have run	rennen
to **see**	saw	have seen	sehen

Annex C

List of vocabulary in alphabetical order (German – English)

Alphabetisches Vokabelverzeichnis (Deutsch – Englisch)

Deutsch	**English**
A	
Abendessen	dinner
Abkürzung	abbreviation
ablösen	relieve (to, r)
ähnlich, gleichartig	similar
allerhöchst	utmost
am Lager	in stock
amtlich, offiziell	official
andeuten	imply (to, r)
annehmen	accept (to, r)
annehmen, einführen	adopt (to, r)
annehmen, vermuten	suppose (to, r)
anrempeln, anstoßen	bump (to, r)
Anrufbeantworter	Answering machine
Antwort	reply
Anzeige, Annonce	advertisement
Arbeitsschicht	shift
Armbanduhr	watch
Arztpraxis	surgery
aufstapeln	pile (to, r)
auftauchen	turn up (to, r)

ausgeben	issue (to, r)
Ausgleich	compensation
ausreichend	sufficient
Ausbildungsverhältnis	apprenticeship
Auszubildende/r	apprentice

B

Banknote zu 5 Pfund	fiver
bar bezahlen	pay cash (to, r)
Barren aus Edelmetall	ingot
Baumarkt	D.I.Y. store
Bausparkasse	building society
befallen	infested
begleiten	accompany (to, r)
beherrschen	dominate (to, r)
beibehalten	retain (to, r)
beklagen	moan (to, r)
Belegschaft/Personal	personnel
Belegschaft/Personal	staff
bequem	comfortable
bereitstellen	provide (to, r)
Berufsschule	vocational training college
beschweren	complain (to, r)
besetzen (Arbeitsplatz)	man (to, r)
Bestandsaufnahme, Inventur	stocktaking
Beutel	pouch
Bezeichnung	designation
Bier, dunkles	bitter
bleiben	stay (to, r)
Bratwürstchen	sausage
Brite, Einwohner von GB	Briton
Bürste, Handfeger, Pinsel	brush

C

City, die /das Finanzviertel von London	City, the

D

Daumen	thumb
Doppelhaushälfte	semi-detached house
Durchschnitt	average
Dünger	fertilizer
dürfen	be allowed to (to)

E

echt	genuine
eifrig	eager
eifrig, begeistert	keen
Eigenname	proper name
Eindruck	impression
Eingangsbereich des Marktes	lobby
eingeben (i.d.B.v.)	enter (to, r)
einen Tag frei haben	day off; to have a day off
Einzelheit	detail
ekelhaft	disgusting
entfernen	remove (to, r)
Entscheidung	decision
entschuldigen	Apologize (to, r)
entspannen	relax (to, r)
entsprechend	appropriate
enttäuscht	disappointed
entwerfen	design (to,r)
erfahren	experienced
Erfahrung	experience
erfinden	invent (to, r)
erfreulich	pleasant
erklären	explain (to, r)
erklären	explain (to, r)
erkunden	explore (to, r)
erleichtert sein	relieved (to be)
erschaffen	create (to, r)
ersetzen	replace (to, r)
Erster Mai; Tag der Arbeit	Labour Day
Essbesteck	cutlery

Essen	nosh (U)
Etikett	label
etwas entsorgen	dispose of s.th. (to, r)

F

Fabrik	factory
Fäulnis	rot
Feierabend machen (U)	knock off (to, r)
Feigling	coward
Feuerwehr	fire brigade
Finanzchef	CFO
Fliege	fly
Fliesen, Kacheln	tiles
fließend	fluently
Flublatt	flyer
Form	shape
freie Stelle (i.d.B.v.)	vacancy
fremd, ausländisch	foreign
Fremder, Ausländer	foreigner
Fremdsprachenkorrespond-ent/in	business correspondent
Fruchtfliege	fruit fly

G

ganz, vollständig, gesamt	entire
Garnison, mil. Standort	garrison
Gebühr	fee
Geduld	patience
Gegenstück	equivalent
Geld ausgeben, Zeit verbringen	spend (to, ir)
Geldautomat	ATM
Geldbetrag (i.d.B.v.)	amount
Geldschein	banknote
Gelegenheit (günstige)	occasion
Gelegenheit	opportunity
genießen	enjoy (to, r)

genormt	standardized
gesamt, alles	entire
Geschäftsführer	CEO
gesetzlicher Feiertag	public holiday
Gesundheitgefahr	health hazard
Gesundheitszeugnis	health certificate
Gewicht	weight
Girokonto	current account
groß (adj.)(i.d.B.v.)	major
Großbuchstabe	capital letter
gründen	found (to, r)
Grundzahl	cardinal number

H

Hacke	hoe
Halbtagsarbeit	half-time job
Haltbarkeit	shelf life
Handel treiben mit	deal in (to)
Handwagen	platform trolley
Harke, Rechen	rake
Heimweh haben	feel homesick (to)
Himmelfahrt	Ascension Day
Holzkiste	wooden crate
Hühnersuppe mit Curry (indisch)	Mulligatawny soup

I

Innenstadt, Großstadt	city
Internat	boarding school

J

jedes 2. Wochenende	every other weekend
jmd. stark beschäftigen	keep someone busy
jmd. "zusammenstauchen" (U)	tell someone off (to)
jmd. überreden	talk s.o. into s.th. (to)
Jungpfadfinderin	Brownie (to, r)

K

Kakerlake	cockroach
Kante	edge
Kaserne	barracks
Kasse abstimmen	balance (to, r)
Kassenbestand	balance (the)
Kassenzettel, Quittung	receipt
Klammer, in Klammern	in brackets
klingeln	ring (to, r)
knusprig	crispy
Kochrezept	recipe
Kofferraum (i.d.B.v.)	boot
Kohlweißling (Schmetterling)	cabbage white butterfly
Konkurrent	competitor
konkurrierend	competing
Kontoführungsgebühr	service charges
Kopfrechnen	mental arithmetic
krankgeschrieben sein	sick leave (to be on)
Kredit	loan
kühl	chilly
Kumpel, Freund	mate (U)
kurz	brief

L

Ladegerät	charger
Lagerhaus	warehouse
Larve	grub
Lastwagen	lorry
Laufband a.d. Kasse	conveyor band
Laune	temper
Lebensmittel (das einzelne)	foodstuff
leicht verderblich	perishable
Leiter	manager
locken	lure (to, r)

M

Made	maggot
Mantel; hier: Kittel	coat

Mass	measure
Mehlwurm	meal worm
Mehrzahl von "penny"	pence
Meinung	opinion
melden, berichten	report (to, r)
Menge	quantity
merkwürdig	strange
mieten	rent (to, r)
Minutenzeiger, großer Zeiger	minute hand
mit etwas vertraut sein	familiar with s.th. (to be)
mit jmd. sprechen	have word with s.o. (to)
mit Wirkung vom	wef (abbr.; with effect from)
Münze	coin
Muskelkater	muscle ache

N

nachfüllen, auffüllen	replenish (to, r)
Nachmittagsmahlzeit (meist warm)	tea
Nachricht	message
Nacktschnecke	slug
Netz	mesh bag
Niedersachsen	Lower Saxony
Norm	standard
normen	standardize (to, r)

O

oben erwähnt; vorher beschrieben	above mentioned
offensichtlich	obviously
öffentliche Verkehrsmittel	public transport
Ohrenkneifer, Ohrwurm	earwig
Ordnungszahl	ordinal number

P

pendeln	commute (to, r)
Pendler	commuter
Personalchef	CPO

Personalchef	CSO
persönlich	personal
Pfadfinder	Scout
Pfand	deposit
Pfingsten	Whitsun
Pinte (ca. 0,56 l)	pint
prakt. Arzt, Allgemeinmediziner	physician
Prospekt	leaflet
pünktlich	in time, on time

R

Rasenmäher	lawn mower
Raupe	caterpillar
regelmäßiges Verb	regular verb
Regen; aus dem Regen in die Traufe	out of the frying pan, into the fire
Regenschauer (i.d.B.v.)	shower
Regenschirm	umbrella
Registrierkasse	cash register
Reisetasche	holdall
reiten; hier: Fahrrad fahren	ride (to, ir)
Rindfleisch- und Nierenpastete	steak & kidney pie
Rindfleisch- und Pilzpastete	steak & mushroom pie
Rückenschmerzen	backache

S

Saatgut, Samen	seeds
Salzstreuer	salt cellar
sammeln, zusammenbringen	gather (to, r)
Satz	sentence
Sauberkeit	cleanliness
Schale	tray
Schichtführer/in	shift supervisior
Schichtplan, Dienstplan	shift roster
Schimmel	mould

schlechte Laune	bad mood
Schmuck, Juwelen	jewellery
schottische Graupensuppe	Scotch broth
Schublade	drawer
Schweiß	sweat (the)
Schwerpunkt	emphasis
schwierig	difficult
Selbstvertrauen	self-confidence
sich krankmelden	report sick (to, r)
sich um etwas kümmern	deal with (to)
Silvester	New Year's Eve
Sonderangebot	special offer
sorgen, sich …	worry (to, r)
Soßenpulver für Vanillesoße	custard powder
Spankiste	small crate
Sparkonto	savings account
Spaten	spade
speziell, besonders	particular
Stadtrand	outskirts (the)
Stange, Barren	bar
stapeln übereinander legen	pile (to, r)
Stapel	pile
stechen	sting (to, ir)
stolz	proud
streiten	argue (to, r)
Strichcode	bar code
Stundenzeiger, kleiner Zeiger	hour hand

T

Tag der Deutschen Einheit	Reunification Day
technischer Leiter	CTO
Telefonhörer	receiver
Tennisschläger	racket
Termin; hier: Arzttermin	appointment
tödlich	fatal

U

überfüllt durch viele Menschen	crowded
überglücklich sein	over the moon (to be)
überrascht sein	surprised (to be)
übertragen	transfer (to, r)
Uhr	clock
Uhrzeiger (i.d.B.v.)	hands
unmittelbar, sofort	immediately
unregelmäßig	irregular
unregelmäßiges Verb	irregular verb
unterscheiden	differ (to, r)
unterscheiden	distinguish (to, r)

V

verantwortlich sein für etwas	be in charge of s.th. (to)
Vereinigtes Königreich	U.K. = United Kingdom
Verfahren	procedure
Verfallsdatum	sell-by date
verlieren	lose (to, ir)
vermeiden	avoid (to, r)
verschmutzen	soil (to, r)
versetzen	post (to, r)
Versorgung, Nachschub, Nachlieferung	supply
verteilen	distribute (to, r)
vertraut machen	familiarize (to, r)
verwesen	decay
vielfach, vielfältig	manifold
Vorname	Christian name
Vorrichtung, Ding, Gerät	device
vorstellen, einführen	introduce (to)

W

wachsen	grow (to, r)
Währung	currency
Wartung	maintenance
Wechsel	change

weggehen wie warme Semmeln	sell like hot cakes (to)
wehtun, schmerzen (aus d. Körper)	ache (to, r)
Weißwein (dt.) aus Rheinhessen	Hock
Werbung	advertising
werden	become (to, ir)
Wespe	wasp
widerlich	disgusting
winzig	tiny
Wohnung (in GB meist Mietwohnung)	flat
Wölfling (Jungpfadfinder)	Wolf Cub
Wurm	worm

Z

Zahlung	payment
Ziffernblatt (i.d.B.v.)	dial
Zischen	hissing sound
zögern	hesitate (to, r)
zufrieden	satisfied
zum Beispiel	e.g. - for example
zuversichtlich	confident
zurückgeben (i.d.B.v.)	return (to, r)
Zweck	purpose
zweisprachig	bilingual
Zweiter Weihnachtstag	Boxing Day

Annex C

List of vocabulary in alphabetical order (English – German)

Alphabetisches Vokabelverzeichnis (Englisch – Deutsch)

English	**Deutsch**

A

abbreviation	Abkürzung
above mentioned	oben erwähnt; vorher beschrieben

accept (to, r)	annehmen
accompany (to, r)	begleiten
ache (to, r)	wehtun, schmerzen (aus d. Körper)
adopt (to, r)	annehmen, einführen
advertisement	Anzeige, Annonce
advertising	Werbung
amount	hier: Geldbetrag
answer phone	Anrufbeantworter
Apologize (to, r)	entschuldigen
appointment	Termin; hier: Arzttermin
apprentice	Auszubildende/r
apprenticeship	das Ausbildungsverhältnis
appropriate	entsprechend
argue (to, r)	hier: streiten
Ascension Day	Himmelfahrt
ATM	Geldautomat
average	Durchschnitt
avoid (to, r)	vermeiden

B

backache	Rückenschmerzen
bad mood	schlechte Laune
balance	Kassenbestand
balance (to, r)	Kasse abstimmen
bar	Stange, Barren
bar code	Strichcode
barracks	Kaserne
be in charge of s.th. (to)	für etwas verantwortlich sein
become (to, ir)	werden
bilingual	zweisprachig
bitter	dunkles Bier
boarding school	Internat
boot	hier: Kofferraum
Boxing Day	2. Weihnachtstag
brackets, in brackets	in Klammern
brief	kurz

Briton	Brite, Einwohner von GB
Brownie	Jungpfadfinderin
brush	Bürste, Handfeger, Pinsel
building society	Bausparkasse
bump (to, r)	anrempeln, anstoßen
business correspondent	Fremdsprachenkorrespondent/in

C

cabbage white butterfly	Kohlweißling (Schmetterling)
capital letter	Großbuchstabe
cardinal number	Grundzahl
cash register	Registrierkasse
caterpillar	Raupe
CEO	Geschäftsführer
CFO	Finanzchef
change	Wechsel
charger	Ladegerät
chilly	kühl
Christian name	Vorname
city	Innenstadt; Großstadt
City, the	das Finanzvirtel von London
cleanliness	Sauberkeit
clock	die Uhr/die große Uhr
coat	Mantel; hier: Kittel
cockroach	Kakerlake
coin	Münze
comfortable	bequem
commute (to, r)	pendeln
commuter	Pendler
compensation	Gelegenheit
competing	konkurrierend
competitor	Konkurrent
complain (to, r)	beschweren
confident	zuversichtlich
conveyor band	Laufband a.d. Kasse
coward	Feigling
CPO	Personalchef

Vocabulary

create (to, r)	erschaffen
crispy	knusprig
crowded	überfüllt durch viele Menschen
CSO	Personalchef
CTO	technsicher Leiter
currency	Währung
current account	Girokonto
custard powder	Soßenpulver für Vanillesoße
cutlery	Essbesteck

D

D.I.Y. store	Baumarkt
day off; have a day off (to)	einen Tag frei haben
deal in (to)	Handel treiben mit
deal with (to)	sich um etwas kümmern
decay (to, r)	verwesen
decision	entscheidung
deposit	Pfand
design (to,r)	hier: entwerfen
designation	Bezeichnung
detail	Einzelheit
device	Vorrichtung, Ding, Gerät
dial	Ziffernblatt
dial	hier: Ziffernblatt der Uhr
differ (to, r)	unterscheiden
difficult	schwierig
dinner	Abendessen
disappointed	enttäuscht
disgusting	widerlich, ekelhaft
dispose of s.th. (to, r)	etwas entsorgen
distinguish (to)	unterscheiden
distribute (to, r)	verteilen
dominate (to, r)	beherrschen
drawer	Schublade

E

e.g. – for example	zum Beispiel

eager	eifrig
earwig	Ohrenkneifer, Ohrwurm
edge	Kante
emphasis	Schwerpunkt
enjoy (to, r)	genießen
enter (to, r)	hier: eingeben
entire	gesamt, alles
equivalent	Gegenstück
every other weekend	jedes 2. Wochenende
experience	Erfahrung
experienced	erfahren
explain (to, r)	erklären
explore (to, r)	erkunden

F

factory	Fabrik
familiar with s.th. (to be)	mit etwas vertraut sein
familiarize (to, r)	vertraut machen
fatal	tödlich
fee	Gebühr
fertilizer	Dünger
fire brigade	Feuerwehr
fiver	Banknote zu 5 Pfund
flat	Wohnung, in GB meist Mietwohnung
fluently	fließend
fly	Fliege
flyer	Flugblatt
foodstuff	das einzelne Lebensmittel
foreign	fremd, ausländisch
foreigner	Fremder, Ausländer
found (to, r)	gründen
fruit fly	Fruchtfliege

G

galore	in Hülle und Fülle
garrison	Garnison, mil. Standort

Vocabulary

gather (to, r)	sammeln, zusammenbringen
genuine	echt
grow (to, r)	wachsen
grub	Larve

H

half-time job	Halbtagsarbeit
hands	hier: Uhrzeiger
have word with s.o. (to)	mit jmd. sprechen
health certificate	Gesundheitszeugnis
health hazard	Gesundheitsgefahr
health insurance	Krankenkasse
hesitate (to, r)	zögern
hissing sound	Zischen
Hock	dt. Weißwein aus Rheinhessen
hoe	Hacke
holdall	Reisetasche
homesick (to feel)	Heimweh haben
hour hand	Stundenzeiger, kleiner Zeiger

I

immediately	unmittelbar, sofort
imply (to, r)	andeuten
impression	Eindruck
in stock	am Lager
in time	pünktlich
infested	befallen
ingot	Barren aus Edelmetall
introduce (to, r)	vorstellen, einführen
invent (to, r)	erfinden
irregular	unregelmäßig
irregular verb	unregelmäßiges Verb
issue (to, r)	ausgeben

J

jewellery	Schmuck, Juwelen

K

keen	eifrig, begeistert
keep someone busy (to)	jemanden stark beschäftigen
knock off (to, r)	Feierabend machen (U)

L

label	Etikett
Labour Day	1. Mai; Tag der Arbeit
lawn mower	Rasenmäher
leaflet	Prospekt
loan	Kredit
lobby	der Eingangsbereich des Marktes
lorry	Lastwagen
lose (to, ir)	verlieren
Lower Saxony	Niedersachsen
lure (to, r)	locken

M

maggot	Made
maintenance	Wartung
major	hier: groß (adj.)
man (to, r)	besetzen (Arbeitsplatz)
manager	Leiter
manifold	vielfach, vielfältig
mate (U)	Kumpel, Freund
meal worm	Mehlwurm
measure	Mass
mental arithmetic	Kopfrechnen
mesh bag	Netz
message	Nachricht
minute hand	Minutenzeiger, großer Zeiger
moan (to, r)	beklagen
mould	Schimmel
Mulligatawny soup	ind. Hühnersuppe mit Curry
muscle ache	Muskelkater

N

New Year's Eve	Silvester

nosh (U)	Essen

O

obviously	offensichtlich
occasion	Gelegenheit
official	amtlich, offiziell
on time	pünktlich
opinion	Meinung
opportunity	Gelegenheit
ordinal number	Ordnungszahl
out of the frying pan, into the fire	aus dem Regen in die Traufe
outskirts	Stadtrand
over the moon (to be)	überglücklich sein

P

particular	speziell, besonders
patience	Geduld
pay cash (to ...)	bar bezahlen
payment	Zahlung
pence	Mehrzahl von "penny"
perishable	leicht verderblich
personal	persönlich
personnel	Belegschaft/Personal
physician	prakt. Arzt, Allgemeinmediziner
pile	der Stapel
pile (to, r)	aufstapeln
pint	Pinte (ca. 0,56 l)
platform trolley	Handwagen
pleasant	erfreulich
post (to, r)	versetzen
pouch	Beutel
procedure	Verfahren
proper name	Eigenname
proud	stolz
provide (to, r)	bereitstellen
public holiday	gesetzlicher Feiertag

public transport	öffentliche Verkehrsmittel
purpose	Zweck

Q

quantity	Menge

R

racket	Tennisschläger
rake	Harke, Rechen
receipt	Kassenzettel, Quittung
receiver	Telefonhörer
recipe	Kochrezept
regular verb	regelmäßiges Verb
relax (to, r)	entspannen
relieve (to, r)	ablösen
relieved (to be)	erleichtert sein
remove (to, r)	entfernen
rent (to, r)	mieten
replace (to, r)	ersetzen
replenish (to, r)	nachfüllen, auffüllen
reply	Antwort
report (to, r)	melden, berichten
report sick (to, r)	sich krankmelden
retain (to, r)	beibehalten
return (to, r)	hier: zurückgeben
Reunification Day	Tag der Deutschen Einheit
ride (to, ir)	reiten; hier: Fahrrad fahren
ring (to, r)	klingeln
rot	Fäulnis

S

s.th. is on special offer	etwas ist im Sonderangebot
salt cellar	Salzstreuer
satisfied (to be)	zufrieden
sausage	Bratwürstchen
savings account	Sparkonto
Scotch broth	schottische Graupensuppe

Scout	Pfadfinder
seeds	Saatgut, Samen
self-confidence	Selbstvertrauen
sell like hot cakes (to)	weggehen wie warme Semmeln
sell-by date	Verfallsdatum
semi-detached house	Doppelhaushälfte
sentence	Satz
service charges	Kontoführungsgebühr
shape	Form
shelf life	Haltbarkeit
shift	Arbeitsschicht
shift roster	Schichtplan, Dienstplan
shift supervisior	Schichtführer/in
shower	hier: Regenschauer
sick leave (to be on)	krankgeschrieben sein
similar	ähnlich, gleichartig
slug	Nacktschnecke
small crate	Spankiste
soil (to, r)	verschmutzen
spade	Spaten
special offer	Sonderangebot
spend (to, ir)	Geld ausgeben, Zeit verbringen
staff	Belegschaft/Personal
Standardize (to, r)	normen
standardized	genormt
stay (to, r)	bleiben
steak & kidney pie	Rindfleisch- und Nierenpastete
steak & mushroom pie	Rindfleisch- und Pilzpastete
sting (to, ir)	stechen
stocktaking	Bestandsaufnahme, Inventur
strange	merkwürdig
sufficient	ausreichend
supply	Versorgung, Nachschub, Nachlief.
suppose (to, r)	annehmen, vermuten
surgery	Arztpraxis
surprised (to be)	überrascht sein

sweat (the)	Schweiß

T

talk s.o. into s.th. (to ...)	jmd. überreden
tea	hier: warme Nachmittagsmahlzeit
tell s.o. off (to)	jmd. "zusammenstauchen" (U)
temper	Laune
thumb	Daumen
tiles	Fliesen, Kacheln
tiny	winzig
to be allowed to	dürfen
transfer (to, r)	übertragen
tray	Schale
turn up (to, r)	auftauchen

U

U.K. = United Kingdom	Vereinigtes Königreich
umbrella	Regenschirm
utmost	allerhöchst

V

vacancy	hier: freie Stelle
vocational training college	Berufsschule

W

warehouse	Lagerhaus
wasp	Wespe
watch	Armbanduhr
wef (abbr.; with effect from)	mit Wirkung vom
weight	Gewicht
Whitsun	Pfingsten
Wolf Cub	Wölfling (Jungpfadfinder)
wooden crate	Holzkiste
worm	Wurm
worry (to , r)	sich sorgen